The Dadian @ 25

Gallery Exhibitions 1989 - 2014

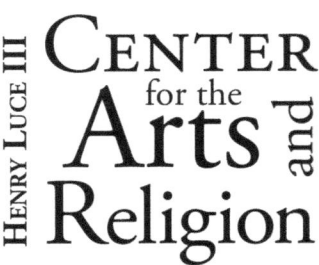

HENRY LUCE III CENTER for the Arts and Religion

The Dadian @ 25: Gallery Exhibitions 1989 – 2014
Trudi Y. Ludwig, Editor and Curator
Dr. Deborah Sokolove, Editor
Amy E. Gray, Book Designer
Narae Kim, Research Assistant

Celebrating 25 years of excellence in the Dadian Gallery
Wesley Theological Seminary
4500 Massachusetts Ave. NW
Washington, DC 20016

Visit us on line at www.wesleyseminary.edu/dadian
or like us on Facebook at:
Henry Luce III Center for the Arts and Religion

Available from Amazon.com, CreateSpace.com,
and other retail outlets

The Dadian @ 25

Gallery Exhibitions 1989 - 2014

A Calling

How bereft we would be without our Dadian Gallery. Gratuitous by nature, the art works exhibited bear within themselves their own confirmation. After their appearance, we recognize we need them. Great works might even leave us wondering how we ever lived without them.

How privileged to wander past our gallery windows catching sight of the mysteries within. Glimpses of evocations of meaning making opportunities arrest our attention, pique interest, startle our awareness, arouse our curiosity or, heaven help us, agitate by confrontation! Such are the ways of the works within.

How compelling when our gallery doors beckon entry. We sense that the inside space is transformed into sacred space. Iconic works artfully hung conspire with our gallery's masterful design to actualize the language of Incarnation through material means. In a community where the written word dominates, where the story of God's saving action is voiced in a myriad of classroom contexts, our gallery exhibitions proclaim visually. Through aesthetic experience, we can engage in an instance of seeing theologically.

How disruptive our gallery contents when confronted by students for whom visual vocabulary and syntax is alien. Yet our persistent and prudent exhibitions remind us that: seeing is a primary human sensibility; seeing substantive works revealing truthful essences belong in religious contexts; and perhaps our seeing is distorted by the rampant plethora of trivial, depersonalized, and often degrading images emerging in technological culture.

How inviting is the notion STOP, SEE, and BE
—the mandate our gallery imposes upon us.

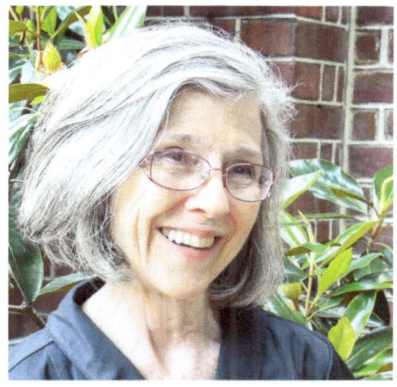

Photo curtesy of Alison Burdett

Catherine Kapikian

Founder and Director,
Henry Luce III Center
for the Arts and Religion
1983 – 2008
Founder,
Dadian Gallery, 1989
Distinguished
Artist-In-Residence
2009 – Present

Clay Bodies, 2006

A History of the Arthur and Marjorie Dadian Gallery

The day after she graduated from Wesley in 1979 with a Master in Theological Studies degree, Catherine Kapikian marched into the dean's office and proposed the establishment of an artist-in-residence at the seminary. The following history of the establishment of the Dadian Gallery is drawn from published writings and an interview with her conducted by Trudi Y. Ludwig in July, 2014.

J. Phillip Wogaman, then dean, and President Jack Knight initially turned me down cold, but eventually responded to my thesis that "without the arts theological education was truncated," by assigning a modest space under the chapel as a studio. They also appointed me to teach a two-credit course in the visual arts. And it was then that I was surprised to realize I had a ministry in the arts on my hands.

I was so convinced of this simple idea, and so passionately invested in doing it, it was a charge, a call. A HUGE call, a mission . . . it's an affliction for God's sake! I was driven, afflicted with a profound sense of ministry and calling on my hands. I looked around, and it was bereft around the country. There was nothing there.

Generally, when seminaries work with the visual arts, they work with them only in terms of products and not the processes undergirding their creation. When they create a space for the works, it's usually a ghettoized space in the library or other building where multiple uses occur. In such situations, the resident community has little understanding, if any, of the processes which undergird the works and make them therefore accessible to understanding. At the very heart of the matter is the issue of understanding the non-verbal vocabulary of the visual which then makes readable the theological proclamation resident in the work.

Using phrases such as "visual theological proclamation" and "authentic engagement with the creative process," Catherine talks about the enthusiastic response to the studio and to her art history course titled "Catacombs to Citicorp." After that first year, the administration was impressed enough to move the studio to the large, central space it now occupies in the Kresge Building. Thus, the arts studio with its open-door policy became an established presence on the Wesley campus.

When Douglass Lewis arrived as president in 1983, he embraced the arts enthusiastically. After considering initiatives that I submitted, he called me to say that he wanted to establish a Center for the Arts and Religion and asked me to direct it.

The next major step in the consolidation of the presence of the arts at Wesley came in 1985. In an overhaul of the curriculum, the faculty, convinced of the role that the imagination can play in theological education, made the critical commitment of requiring each student to take two credits in the arts.

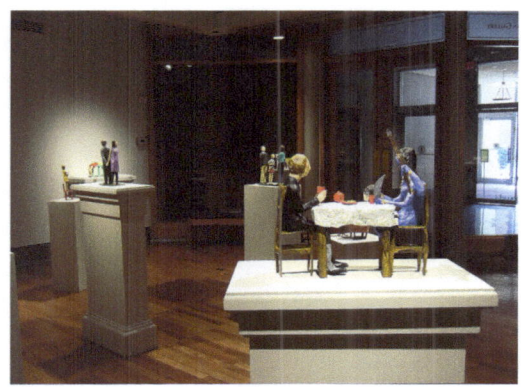

The Paper People, 2012

By the end of the 1980s, the administration made available space for a formal gallery where works done at the intersection of art and religion could be lifted up. Arthur Dadian contributed a major gift that was matched by the seminary for the creation of a state-of-the-art gallery. Named the Dadian Gallery in his honor, it completed the three-part presence of the arts at Wesley: the studio with its resident artists; the center, to integrate the arts into the curriculum; and the gallery. The first show in the gallery honored his generous gift.

At the time there was a Board of Directors for the Center, so I went to my board and said 'we should take $5000 of that $100,000 and we should hire a gallery designer to come forth with some really good ideas.' The board said, "Absolutely not. Let the planners and architects do that." Meanwhile I interviewed the Directors of the Hirshhorn and the National Gallery of Art and wrote a long document on what was essential for a small jewel-like, *quality* gallery. So the last board meeting of the year, which was December, 1988, [the planners and architects] come forth with a plan for the gallery. And they give it to our board. And the board looks at it and accepts it. And I looked at it and said "Oh my God! Washington doesn't need another gallery like this!"

So it's December 22 or 23, and I called up Doug Lewis' office and told his secretary that it's urgent. I said, "Doug, as far as I'm concerned, I want this to go on the books that I think this is an outrageous plan." Because what used to be there was church administration offices. There was a brick wall straight across there! With one door! The brick wall had to come down so that opened eyes could see into that space.

However, the plan presented was shopping mall mentality. Those were the exact words I used with Doug Lewis. He said, "What do you want to do about this?" I said I know a wonderful gallery curator, Marvin Liberman. We should just call him up, and as soon as Christmas is over, you and I ought to sit down with him. And it was terrible for Doug because that meant the plans were not going to go out to be

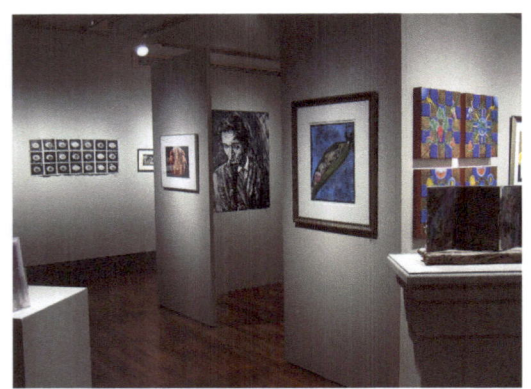

Food and Form, 2010

worked into the general contracting price. That probably would cost more!

Two people resigned from our board because of the autonomy that Doug and I exercised in overriding that decision. So it was a dangerous battle. Doug had wanted to have the gallery included in the total [renovation] package, but it wasn't. He wanted everything to go out on bidding uniformly. But I blew the whistle on the gallery, [and] he had the courage to step out of the box, too. So together we did. Doug Lewis is absolutely essential to the beginning of the Dadian as we know it.

So we call up Marvin, and we all sit down together. And the only thing I told Marvin was that I wanted a higher ceiling in the center, so that part of it could be like a really sacred space. And have moveable walls, which really changes peoples' perspective as they move into the space. And the wonderful glass walls that make the gallery immediately visible when walking into the building. [This was] a rejection of the space planner's shopping mall mentality gallery design. And Doug Lewis risked his neck and supported my rejection. It was his willingness to accept the vision. And that's huge. This is such an important thing, this has meant something to a lot of people. It's a quarter of a century, and it's still here. By God, it really is a call. A deep, overwhelming call. An affliction. But a blessed one.

Following the gallery's construction, it took us several years to work out policies commensurate with our mission and simultaneously our administrative limitations. The gallery design has served us well through the years. Its ever-changing exhibitions have challenged the community with tough questions as well as keen insights.

The history of the Center for the Arts and Religion cannot be fully told without acknowledging the tremendous benefit that has been derived from the infusion of three Luce Foundation grants. These have not only enabled a deepening and an expansion of the program, they have been an affirmation to those pioneers, Catherine Kapikian and Douglass Lewis, that others saw the value of their enterprise. But the fullness of that story is for another time and place, as here we pause to celebrate twenty-five years of exhibitions in the Arthur and Marjorie Dadian Gallery, a jewel box setting for exhibiting the work of artists in all religious traditions and faiths who articulate their spiritual heritage in their work or for whom art is a medium for expressing their faith.

In to the Future

Upon the 2009 retirement of our Founder and long-time Director, Catherine Kapikian, I was invited to lead the Center for the Arts and Religion. After many years as Curator of the Gallery, it was daunting to step into the role that Catherine had defined as artist, as visionary, and as champion of all the arts that have found a place in the midst of Wesley Theological Seminary thanks to her tireless efforts. Since then, I have worked with Amy Gray, our able and devoted Program Administrator, to create and clarify systems and procedures that will help to carry the work of the Center into the future, no matter who bears the title of Director.

One of my first duties as Director was to hire a new Curator, Alexandra Sherman, who served ably through 2012, and then handed over her duties to Trudi Y. Ludwig. Like all of their predecessors, Alexandra and Trudi are working artists, bringing an artist's sensibility not only to the selection of artworks and the design of exhibitions, but also to forging relationships with the artists who entrust their works to us. Watching them work has been an education for me, as well as for the Wesley community at large, as each of them has invited artists from new corners of the art world to bring their work into a place where seminarians, pastors, and scholars live and learn.

As the most immediately visible project of the Center for the Arts and Religion, the Dadian Gallery offers a unique opportunity for artists whose work is excellent but often not widely known. When David McAllister-Wilson became President of the Seminary, he asked that we reserve one work from each show for display on a wall in his office that had been specially fitted with hanging rails, so that he could talk about it with those who came to visit him. This generous gesture is symbolic of the importance that the arts hold here at Wesley Theological Seminary. This exhibition and its accompanying catalog celebrate 25 years of the Seminary's commitment to the notion that the ongoing conversation between artists and theologians requires the physical, and ever changing, presence of excellent art at the heart of the seminary.

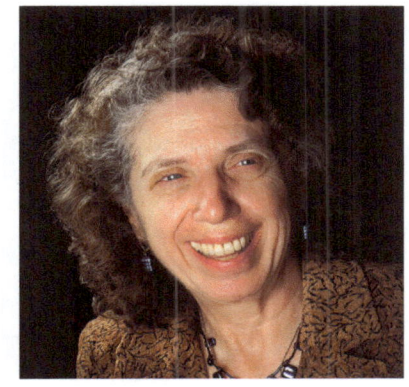

Deborah Sokolove
Director,
Henry Luce III Center
for the Arts & Religion
2009 – Present
Curator, Dadian Gallery
1994 – 2009

1989–1991

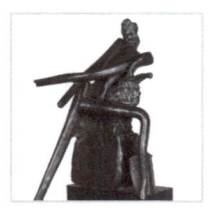

In the Armenian Spirit: Works of the 20th Century
From the Collection of Vartkess and Rita Balian
In Tribute to the Heritage of Arthur and Marjorie Dadian
October 22 – December 7, 1989

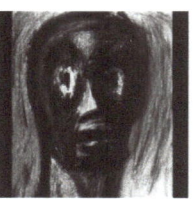

Survivor of Death, Witness to Life – Holocaust Drawings
Gyorgy Kadar
May 8 – June 29, 1990

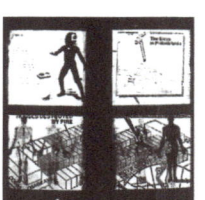

Art and Conscience: Images from the Urban Reality
September 15 – October 27, 1990

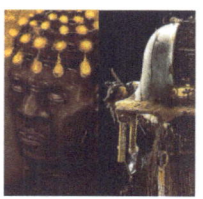

Risk and Integrity: Two Masters from Washington
The Paintings of Robyn Johnson-Ross
The Sculpture of John Dickson
November 10 – December 23, 1990

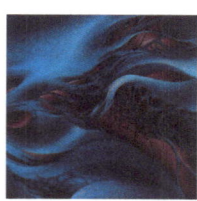

Elemental Forms
Drawings by Marnie Montgomery
January 19 – March 2, 1991

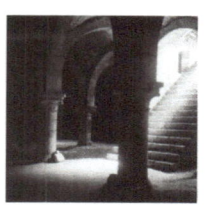

Of Heaven and Earth
Medieval Cathedrals: Through the Eye of the Lens
March 16 – April 11, 1991

I've been asked to reflect on my brief period of work at the Dadian Gallery, which I do with considerable pleasure. Those nearly two years engaged in the gallery's inception, design and then its initial directorship were immensely gratifying to me, and in many ways a heartbreak to have had to leave it so soon.

Given that my first role was as consultant to the architects in the actual design of the future gallery, I found it then an imperative to define how a small space, in the midst of the Seminary's campus, could become a magnet for both seminarians and the general public, in equal measure, to explore the link between the religious life for which the seminary was formed, the public with its broader and often secular concerns, and types of fine art inherently unrelated to religious life—yet containing so many of the threads of human existence that are the substance of art and concern of religious thought. I saw this then as a different form of trinity, if you will, a meeting place between these three forces.

The space itself, because it was so small, needed to present itself as a jewel into which one could quietly be surrounded for a brief period insulated from the outside world. Also, because of its limited size, it needed to be significantly flexible, both in terms of its walls and its lighting, and the kind of interior it could create for each of its exhibitions. Thirdly, we then considered the Dadian to be a fully functioning museum-level exhibition environment, with all its environmental support systems. It's my hope that we achieved all three of these goals.

Once I comprehended the potential of the Dadian, I began to sense what kinds of exhibitions could explore the idea of this secular trinity that so drove my concerns of that time. The Seminary felt comfortable with my suggested role as director, and off we went. In the three exhibits that I fully conceived and curated in that first year (the fourth was a previous commitment to an individual artist close to the Center's community), in each I wanted to touch upon certain vital issues that would allow the general public and seminarians (and the artist community as well) to see a reason for their being exhibited in that moment and at a religious seminary.

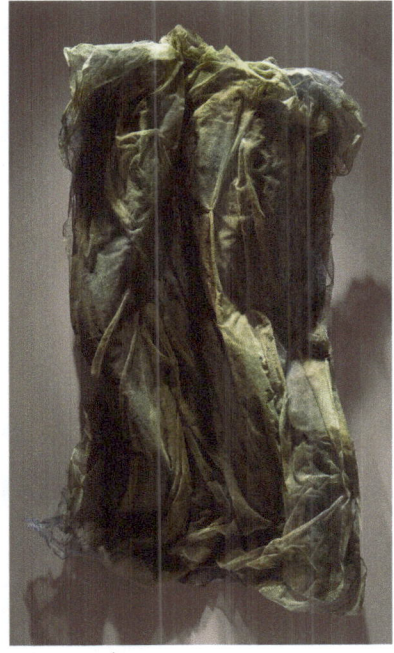

Murmer 4

Marvin Liberman

Curator, 1989 – 1990

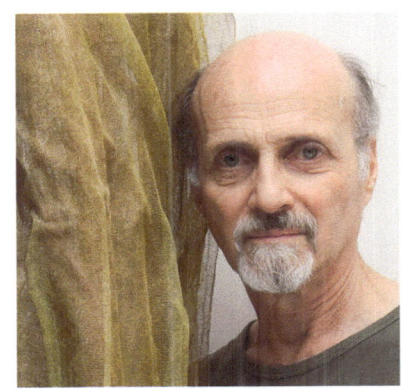

From this came *Art and Conscience*, in which artists visualized the price paid for the intense level of crime, drugs and murder then so much a part of our lives; *Risk and Integrity*, which presented two of Washington's most demanding artists of that moment so as to know how important the content of their work was; and finally *Of Heaven and Earth*, which explored how photography had and still was engaged with Europe's Gothic Cathedrals as a search for meaning within them and their endurance amidst the ever-changing epochs that passed before them to the present day.

All three, as their titles reflect, explore dualities, equal to the dualities between the religious and the secular worlds, and art which hovers always between them, in some way or another. May your center and the Dadian project have yet another 25 years of success and outreach through its programs.

1991-1992

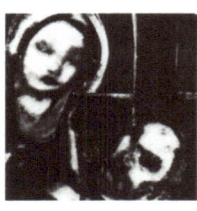

Wrestling with the Angel: Trials and Revelations
Paintings by Grace Hartigan
September 22 – November 22, 1991

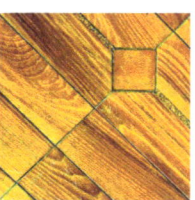

Black History Month: A Special Profile Exhibition
Sauveur Aliance
January 15 – February 7, 1992

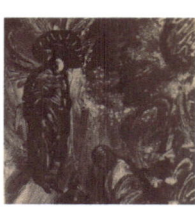

Of Darkness and Light: Fragments from a Pilgrimage
by Constance Pierce
February 23 – March 28, 1992

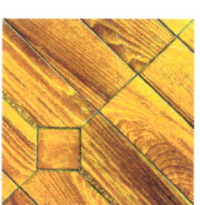

Empowering Monotype
Pyramid Atlantic, W. D. Workshop,
Washington Studio School, Washington Printmakers Gallery
April 12 – May 30, 1992

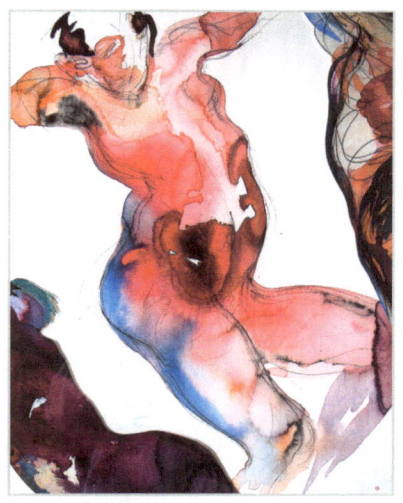

Wounded Souls, Purgatorio

Constance Pierce

Curator, 1991 – 1992
Artist-in-Residence 1990

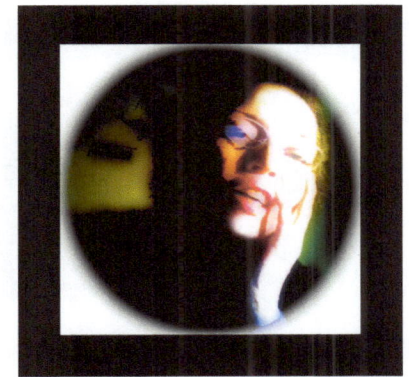

I am compelled by allegorical themes such as pilgrimage, lamentation, absolution, and transcendence. Scriptural narrative, in all of its mythic and consuming drama, reveals to me the ancient parables, reborn in our current world of dissonance and division The moment of betrayal or resurrection is not ancient history, but is enacted anew.

I have a passion for remembering gesture. I want to illuminate the transcendent aspects of life, especially those experiences where we are entrained by a grace beyond ordinary perception. Through expression of both the intimate and expansive—born of both darkness and light—art inspires us to our highest humanity, seeding a metamorphosis.

My time as artist-in-residence at the Henry Luce Center, and as guest curator for the Dadian Gallery, as well as my friendship with distinguished artist, Catherine Kapikian, were life changing events. Those experiences nourished my soul and informed my art for years to come. It was an honor to have my work reviewed in the Washington Post and on WETA-TV as a result of my solo exhibition in the Dadian and the stature of the Luce Center. Both of these are the result of the epiphanic vision of Professor Kapikian.

~ Joy on the 25th Anniversary! ~

1992-1993

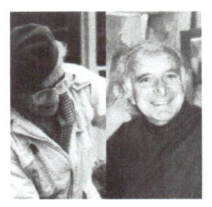

Food for Body and Spirit
Paintings by Sy Gresser & Chaim Nahor
September 20 – October 31, 1992

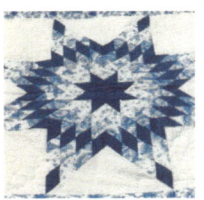

Quilts: Patterns of Faith
A Group Exhibition
February 21 – March 28, 1993

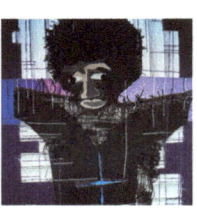

Approach to Calvary
Words and Images of Insight on the Crucifixion
Catherine Kapikian
April 6, 1993 in Oxnam Chapel

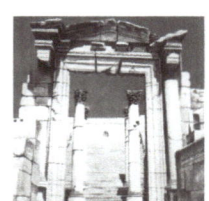

Archaeology and Ancient Jordan
Artifacts from Tell el-Umeiri
April 25 – May 30, 1993

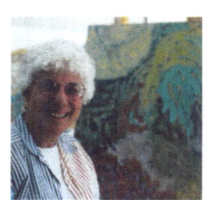

Expression and Revelation: The Artist as Spiritual Messenger
Paintings by Pearl Mandel
June 14 – July 10, 1993

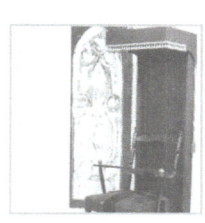

Ex-Cathedra
Selected Works of Bobbie Brooks Crow
July 12 – August 22, 1993

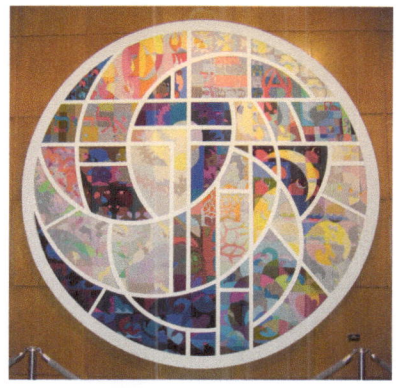

Wood and Tapestry Roundel

Catherine Kapikian

Distinguished
Artist-in-Residence
2008 – Present

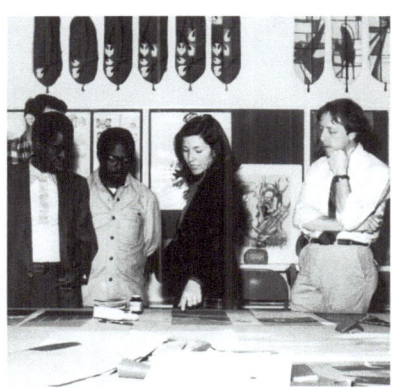

Catherine in the studio with students

Some time ago, I read that "Christian witness is a manifestation of God's creative activity through the expenditure of a human life." This struck a chord in me. I found meaning creating works for communities of faith from a faith point of view. This ongoing consent has become a way of life for me, and often I can't tell the difference between my life and my art.

All worship spaces are unique and none are complete until the assembly gathers. My interest is in this moment. When the prayers are uttered, the songs sung, and the Word heard, the visual accoutrements in the space, in concert with the space itself, serve to place all things together in a dynamic equilibrium.

In my site-specific works, I begin by listening closely to the community's concerns and wishes. Then, I give careful attention to each space's relationship of parts, its sight lines, value contrasts, textural qualities of surfaces, and its colors, hues and intensities. I create relationships of light and dark, mass and void; invent movements of shapes and patterns; and apply color. And, finally, I hope that the resulting configurations of images will bring more acutely into focus the ritual moment. The more complete the visual unity in a space, the more holy the space becomes. I endeavor to achieve such space. And such space awaits community.

This way of working allows the exploration of questions which fascinate me, such as: What does art have to do with religious experience? What does art have to do with the quest for the Holy? How is art related to the questions of life's ultimate meaning?

Artist's statement from *Abiding Presence* exhibition, 1998

1993 – 1994

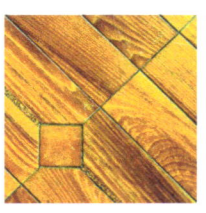

The WTS Community Show
Artists in Residence, Students, Faculty, Staff
September 1 – 30, 1993

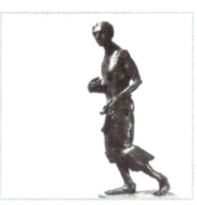

Sculptures in Direct Metal – Expressions of Spirituality
Justo Arosemena
September 26 – October 29, 1993

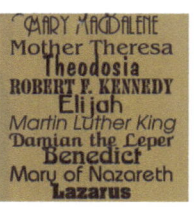

For All the Saints
A Mixed Media Group Exhibition
November 1 – December 11, 1993

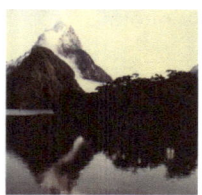

Ancient Prayers and a 20th Century Traveler
Photographs by Lawrence Hull Stookey
November 1 – December 11, 1993
In the Board Room

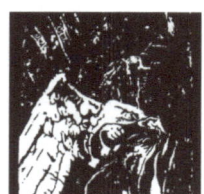

Oil on Canvas: An Ecclesiological Exegetical Commentary in a Prophetic Perspective
Wesley Maxwell Lawton
December 15, 1993 – January 4, 1994

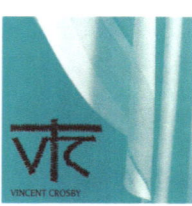

With Heart and Hand: Fabric in the Service of Liturgy
Fr. Vincent Crosby, OSB
January 10 – February 12, 1994

Tear Down These Walls:
A Manifesto for the Reformation of the Gallery Experience

> When artistic objects are separated from both conditions of origin and operation in experience, a wall is built around them that render almost opaque their general significance. John Dewey, *Art as Experience,* 1931

Sometime we marvel that our many years in the graduate theological environment led us to a small frame shop and art gallery in rural Virginia. We are convinced that our experience at Wesley in the classroom, studio, office, and gallery were pivotal in equipping us for our current ministry. The past five years have shaped a new way to look at the art's worth for a community in the relationships that are built, the conversations that the creative imagination helps to foster, and the identity that the arts bring to a community. We have come to understand that art is language … not object. We have come to believe that it is time to rethink the gallery experience and its role in building community.

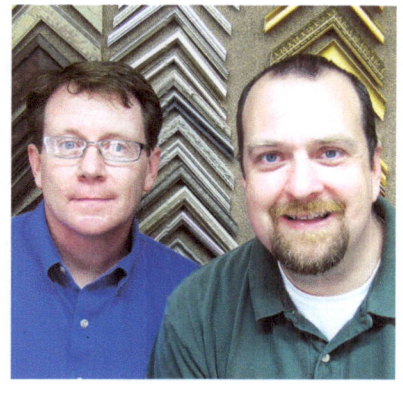

Patrick Ellis
Curator, 1993 – 1994
Exhibition 2005
Artist-in-Residence
1992 – 1993
Mitchell Bond (right)
Registrar, 1998 – 2009

Reflection on the Dadian@25: Twenty-five years is not only an opportunity for celebration, but an invitation for critical reflections on the future. As we celebrate 25 years of the Dadian Gallery bookended between Catherine Kapikian's intuitive vision and Deborah Sokolove's profound theological and pastoral insights we might want to ask why this conversation has not caught fire in a larger context. The apologetics for theology and the arts has changed little in 25 years, and the arts remain mired at the periphery of both theological study and pastoral practice.

Maybe, just maybe, in our desire to celebrate the arts, the pristine gallery experience in fact works to isolate, separate and ultimately truncate the communicative power works of art offer to the community of faith. Too often the gallery experience becomes a place apart, a private and often elitist oratory where individuals are offered little more than quiet moments of aesthetic contemplation. In our well meaning desire to enshrine the art product or celebrate the talent of a few select individuals, have we separated both the artist and their work from the more meaningful ways art can interact within the human experience? If art has transformative powers for the human condition, why do our exhibitions draw such a small percentage of the community?

A seminary scripture or systematic theology class is training ground for mission and evangelism and never meant to be the end product. The classroom experience's ultimate value is not in those concentrated moments of inquiry, but rather in how the experience equips a student for ministry in the real lives of communities and congregations.

Likewise the gallery experience should not be the goal or culmination for artists working at the service of God's people. The product of the creative imagination is about building relationships, fostering conversation and nurturing community. The real value of the artist and the artist's creations is not centered in the object, but rather in the space between the object and the work and lives of the people of God. When we place an object on the wall of a gallery, we truncate its potential and ask it to do something it cannot do alone.

Let us face the challenge together to rethink the gallery experience and find new ways to reconnect the object to its work within the body of Christ.
www.goosecreekstudio.com

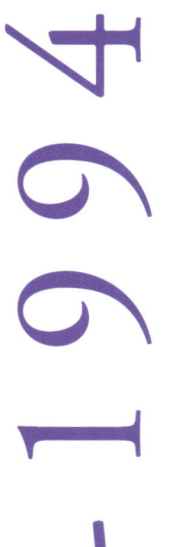

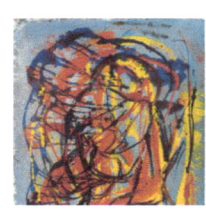

Lenten Meditations
Paintings by Sister Mary Grace, O.P., and Tony Franovic
February 16 – April 1, 1994

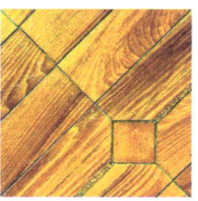

The Art of Buon Fresco
Michael Hearn
April 4 – May 14, 1994
In the Board Room

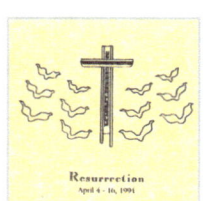

Resurrection
Selected works by Maria Velez
April 4 – April 16, 1994

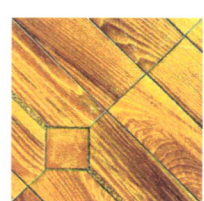

Children's Spiritual Art
Grace Episcopal Day School in Kensington, MD
Designed by Catherine Kapikian
April 18 – April 30, 1994

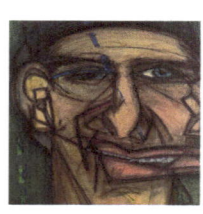

Random 24
Bill Rock
May 2 – May 27, 1994

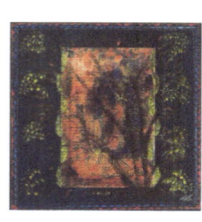

New Icons
Paintings by Deborah Sokolove
June 1 – June 26, 1994

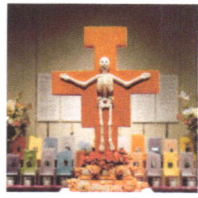

Artists Respond to AIDS
Allen R. Waters and Thomas C. Waters
July 5 – August 26, 1994

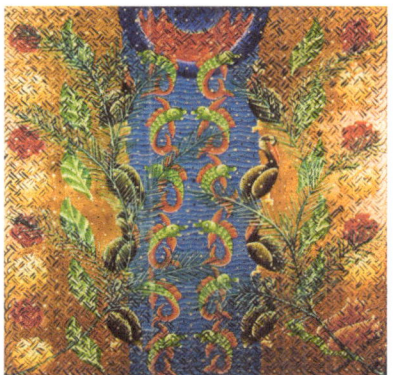
There is a River

Deborah Sokolove
Exhibition 1994
Artist-in-Residence 1994

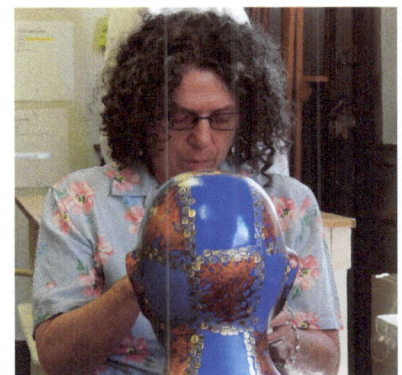

The Center for the Arts and Religion first came to my attention some time in 1993. I had recently moved from Los Angeles to the DC area. I was teaching art in a state university and growing increasingly unhappy with my colleagues' resistance to allowing students to express their religious ideas in their work. The previous summer, I had attended a week-long workshop on art and worship at the Pacific School of Religion. While there, it became clear to me that I was called to something called "arts ministry," but I had no idea what that could mean. So when Catherine Kapikian invited me to come to Wesley as an Artist-in-Residence in January, 1994, I was elated.

That spring, I worked in the studio, experimenting with new materials, new processes, and new ideas. Released from the incessant demands of a full-time teaching load, and now in a place flooded with both spiritual and literal light, I found a freedom to explore visually as well as intellectually the religious ideas that were filling my imagination. Traditional images of saints were juxtaposed with maps and photographs of storefront churches, all twining around the Tree of Life and overlaid with intricate interlace patterns drawn from Celtic and Islamic visual vocabularies.

In June of that year, Patrick Ellis, then the Curator of the Dadian Gallery, installed these images in what was to be his last exhibition in that role. Upon his resignation, I was invited to serve as Curator, which position I held for fifteen years. During that time, I took enough classes at Wesley to earn the Master of Theological Studies degree and went on to earn a PhD in liturgical studies at Drew University. Although I long ago moved my art practice out of the Wesley studio, I continue to paint and exhibit, incorporating some of the visual language of the icon tradition as well as other theological and liturgical motifs into my continually developing style.

www.dsokolove.com

1994–1995

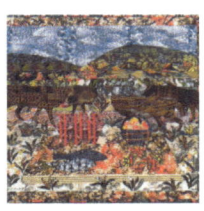

Themes in Biblical Hospitality
Exhibition of Art Quilts by Lee Porter
August 31 – October 1, 1994

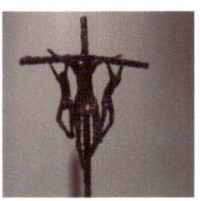

Expressions of Faith and a Marginalized Existence
A Juried Show
October 17 – December 16, 1994

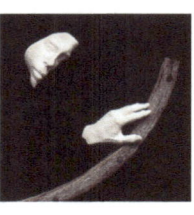

Hand and Soul
Mixed Media Sculpture by Martha Tabor
January 9 – February 24, 1995

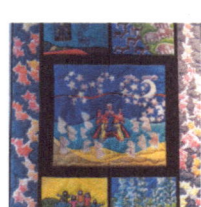

Seeing the Stories:
Art Quilts based on Stories from Hebrew Scripture
Students in the 1993-1994 art classes at Saint Francis Xavier School
January 15 – February 20, 1995
In the Board Room

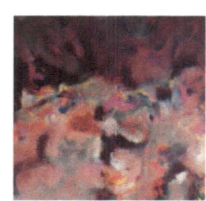

Artists-In-Residence: Selected Works
Patrick Ellis, Toni Franovic, Kathy Keler,
Doug Purnell, and Hija Yu
May 5 – June 9, 1995

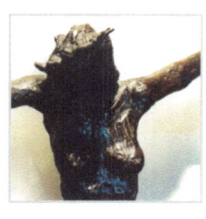

Crucifixion of the Feminine
A Group Exhibition
Guest Curator, Martha Mabey
June 19 – August 18, 1995

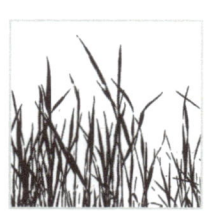

Kansas Farm Women: Growing Out of the Tilth
Photographer Cynthia Vagnetti
June 19 – August 18, 1995
In the Board Room

In Memoriam

Martha Tabor was a beloved member of the Washington, DC art community. Her 1995 exhibition in the Dadian Gallery consisted of eleven carefully-crafted, evocative sculptures made of found objects, cloth, pieces of curly willow, and hydrocal castings of faces and hands. At that time, she was just beginning to claim an identity as a sculptor, having previously worked as a documentary photographer and printmaker. This new direction was more poetic, more mysterious, more elliptical than anything she had done previously. In her statement for that show, she wrote:

> My sculpture tends to start from a feeling evoked by the curve of a wagon wheel or a pair of ice tongs or the suggestive curves of curly willow branches. I then work with the pieces until I come to some resolution with the shapes and the feelings that they suggest. I work with both my own face and those of others in making castings. Generally I use my own hands in the pieces since they are most available to me for casting. I've found that hands can have enormous evocative power with only slight shifts in muscle and tension.

When the exhibition was over, Martha continued to feel connected to WTS and the Center, frequently calling or coming in to talk about the new pieces she was working on. As she developed the piece that came to be called "Jacob's Ladder," she began to envision it in the Kresge stairwell where it now resides, a gift to generations of seminarians.

Martha was by nature a quiet person, her generous warmth made evident in proffered cups of tea, in her affection for her dogs, in deep friendships maintained over many years. Her memorial service filled the Washington, DC Friends Meeting House to overflowing as person after person stood to share a tender memory or a funny story about the woman whose life had touched theirs in some way. After the service, the close friends who had sat with her and held her hand as she died, invited everyone into the social hall. There tables were piled high with the photographs and prints Martha had instructed them to give away, her final gifts to those who loved her.

Deborah Sokolove

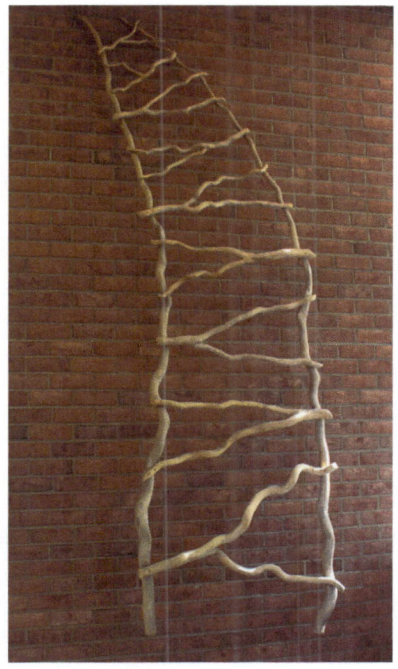

Jacob's Ladder

Martha Tabor
(1940 – 2004)
Exhibition 1995

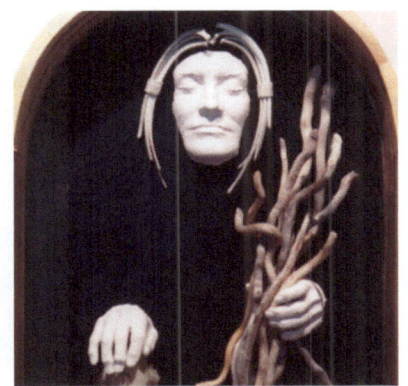

Winter (detail)

1995 - 1996

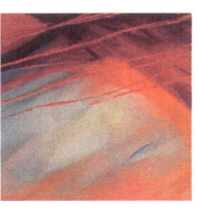

The Color Veiling Journey
Paintings by Barbara Thelin Preston
September 7 – October 13, 1995

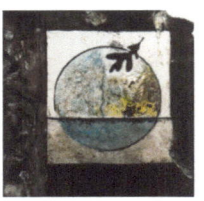

Salus: Raku-Fired Ceramic Wall Panels and Drawings
by Patrick Timothy Caughy
October 30 – December 22, 1995

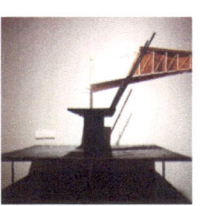

A Quiet Place
A Design Studio
from the University of Virginia School of Architecture
February 5 – March 22, 1996

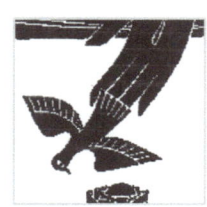

Seeing and Believing
Scratchboard Drawings of Frank Kacmarcik
February 5 – March 22, 1996
In the Board Room

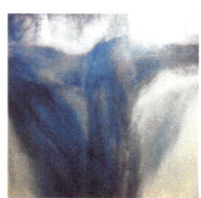

The WTS Community Show
Artists-in-Residence, Students, Faculty, and Staff
April 8 – June 7, 1996

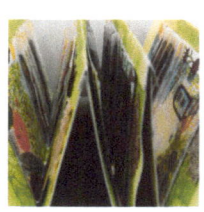

Interior Visions
Ardyth Davis, Terry Hitt, and Ann Zahn
June 24 – August 9, 1996

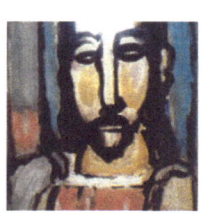

Selected works from the Lady Margretta Jamieson Collection
Paintings, Drawings and Sculptures
August 19 – August 23, 1996

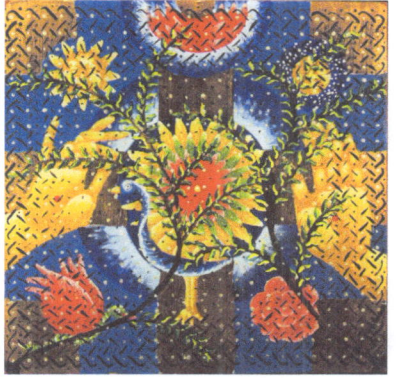

Presence

Deborah Sokolove
Curator, 1994 – 2008

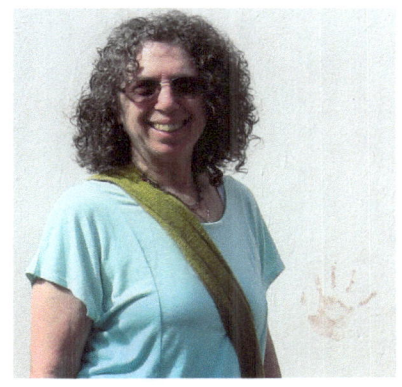

I was the Curator of the Dadian Gallery from June, 1994 until July, 2009. During that time, I mounted over 75 exhibitions, each lasting about six weeks. Today, looking back, my memories are a blur of studio visits, endless correspondence and telephone calls, unpacking crates, working with Randall Adams to install and light each work to its best advantage, hosting receptions, and then taking everything down and packing it up in the strangely empty gallery.

At first, I was so unsure of how to design exhibitions that I built a scale model of the gallery, and printed out small photographs of each piece so that I could figure out where everything went before the work arrived. Eventually, I became so familiar with how to work in that tiny, jewel-box space that I could simply open the crates, lean the work against the walls, and design the show on the fly. A set of movable walls made it possible to redesign the space for each show, creating intimate spaces that encouraged viewing small works at close range, or opening up vistas so that large works could be seen in a single glance. For me, designing exhibitions is itself an art form, a three dimensional collage in which each element must be in conversation with all the others, revealing the creative concerns of the artist and forming an underlying current that carries the viewer from one piece to the next.

The best part of the Curator's job is meeting other artists, hearing them talk about their work, and, when possible, visiting their studios. Over the years I was privileged to get to know artists just beginning their careers, and others who have labored for most of their lives in obscurity. Many of these artists have been explicitly concerned with religious or spiritual themes. For others, the creative process itself is a deeply spiritual experience, a way of being in conscious contact with the divine spark that animates all of us but that is so often difficult to access. For all of them, an exhibition in the Dadian Gallery was an opportunity to present their work in a context where it would be taken seriously both as art and as theology.

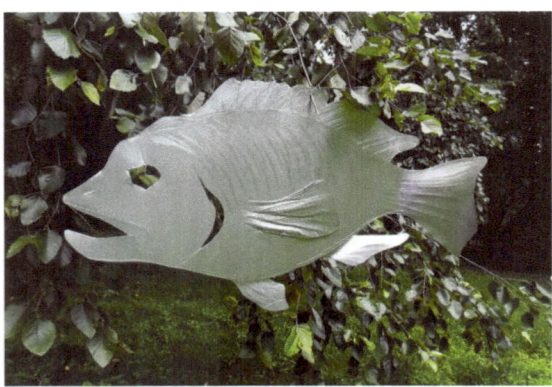

The Fish Tree (detail)

Bill Rock

Exhibition 1994
Artist-in-Residence
1993 – 1994

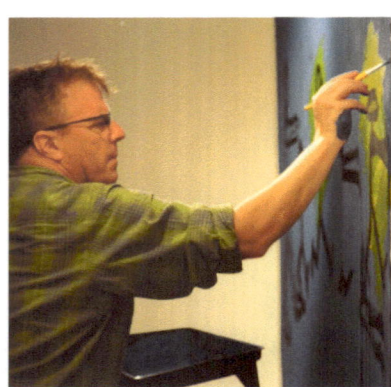

The Artist-in-Residence program at Wesley was one of discovery into my art practice as well as into other artists' work.

Arriving at Wesley Seminary, I had recently completed a body of work consisting of 20+ black, over-sized neckties constructed of cardboard and wire. Each necktie sculpture had a companion drawing (full color) to describe (visually illustrate) the unique characteristics (imbedded but not visible) in the individual sculptural forms. It was a study in the parallel lives that homo sapiens live; the generic, homogenous herd side (the black ties) and in contrast, the unique, one-of-a-kind qualities or gifts that can be attributed to human spirit (the colored companion drawings).

Following a brief transition period in the new studio setting at Wesley, the work shifted to large-scale sculpture, a continuation from the neckties but now using human form (heads). This inspired the next body of work, "Random 24", an examination into first impressions of strangers, which became my residency exhibition at The Dadian Gallery.

The exhibition brochure for "Random 24" explained it this way: "A series of portraits using anonymous persons as subjects. This project was initiated to investigate random encounters with humanity – simple exchanges which occur everyday between strangers."

The residency experience helped me to better understand that spirituality could be found in many forms of art, and in many types of people.

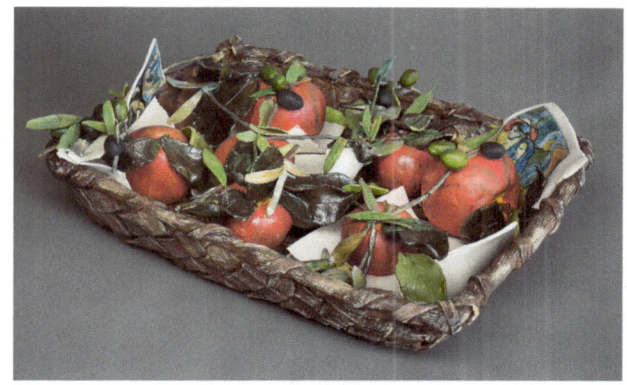

Gardening with Francis

Ginger Henry Geyer
Exhibition 1997

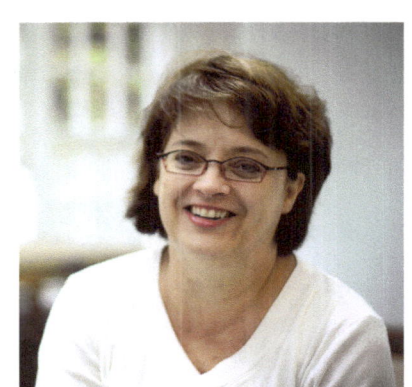

After working in an art museum for a long while, our family moved in 1988. I had majored in painting and got an MFA in museum education, but set aside art-making for 13 years. I knew when I finally committed to it, it would be full steam ahead. I cocooned myself for a couple of years, experimenting and searching for my own way, blasted through the "honeymoon stage" and experienced the existential doubts of claiming to be an artist and a person of faith.

I timidly went to conferences on art and faith, where despite the bewildering atmosphere I managed to show my humble wares to Catherine Kapikian and later, Deborah Sokolove. That led to an offer for an exhibition at the Dadian Gallery in 1997, a most timely and encouraging gift. That show, which we titled *Wholly Porcelain*, opened many doors for me both professionally and personally. It was my third solo exhibition but the first out-of-town one, and the first to be professionally shipped, installed and publicized. I felt an enormous sense of validation of my call as an artist from the community at Wesley. Two major pieces sold, which was a boost. I came up to Washington for the opening and for the closing; those trips to our nation's capitol were quite enriching, as I hit every museum I could. That solidified my hunch to incorporate art history into my own work. Within the year I met a mentor who would be pivotal to my process, Betty Sue Flowers, and I mustered the courage to quit a problematic teaching job in a fundamentalist college. Thanks to Deborah's sage advice, I allowed myself to see art-making as a spiritual discipline, one that would take me on an inner and outer journey I never predicted. I engaged a literary agent, enrolled in seminary, and was taken on by a good, local gallery. And I learned how challenging and rewarding it is to manage family, work, and art-making.

Wholly Porcelain was in many ways the entrée to my artistic career. Over the years, the relationships made there have bloomed, and I am deeply honored to be called back in to celebrate this remarkable 25th anniversary!

1996-1997

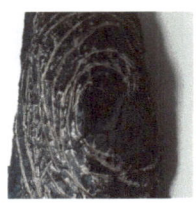

Stations of the Cross
Sculptures and Drawings by Jorge Sardinas
September 3 – October 24, 1996

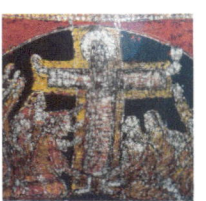

Christian Art from India
The Collection of Naomi Wray
September 3 – October 24, 1996
In the Board Room

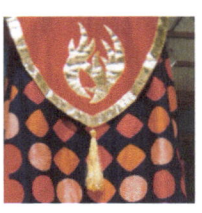

Vessels and Vestments
Contemporary Christian Liturgical Art
November 1 – December 20, 1996

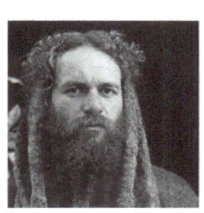

Portraits on the Street
Photographs by Tom Nyerges
November 1 – December 20, 1996
In the Board Room

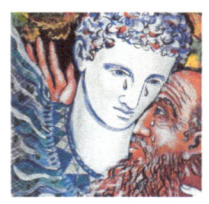

Art for Faith's Sake : Images of the Prodigal Son
From the Collection of Jerry A. Evenrud
February 3 – March 21, 1997

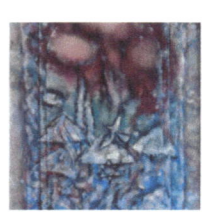

Art in the Seminary: The WTS Community Show
In Memory of Constance Sherridan Hefner
Artists-in-Residence, Students, Staff
March 31 – May 16, 1997

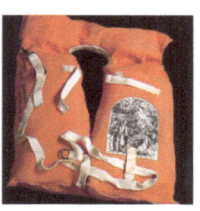

Wholly Porcelain
Sculpture by Ginger Geyer
May 22 – July 3, 1997

**Exhibitions thanks to the generosity
of the Reverend Dr. Winston and Lois Trever
in 2001, 2004, 2007, 2009, 2013**

Trever Bennett was a renowned artist, known for her
watercolors of the desert landscapes of the Southwest.
She grew up in California and knew at an early age
that she wanted to be an artist. After a successful career
in interior design, she became a painter and an art
teacher. In 2005, Trever Bennett passed away at the
age of 89, after many years as a resident of Apple Valley
in San Bernadino County, California.

In 1997, her brother, the Reverend Dr. Winston Trever, and his wife
Lois wanted to commemorate Trever's talent and commitment to
the arts. They established an arts endowment at Wesley Theological
Seminary in honor of Trever, which has funded a series of exhibitions
of landscape paintings. An avid photographer, Winston understood
the importance of using visual media to bring the world to others.
The gift he and Lois gave to support the Henry Luce III Center
for the Arts and Religion here at Wesley ensures that the dialogue
between artists and theologians continues.

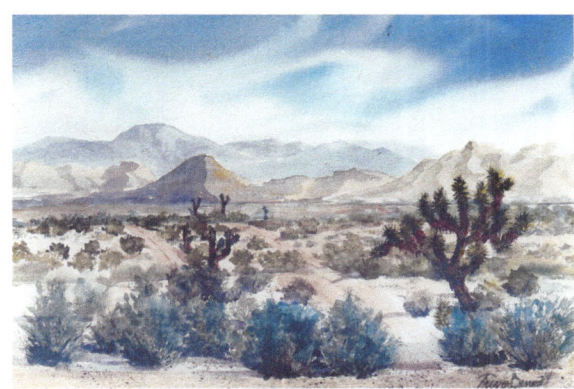

My Painting View

In Honor of
Trever Bennett
Exhibition 1998

**Exhibitions thanks to the generosity of Tom and Jean Hefner
in 1997, 2003, 2008, 2010, 2012**

We are grateful to Tom and Jean Hefner for their generous support
that made these exhibitions possible. Long time friends of Wesley
and patrons of the arts, Tom and Jean saw the opportunity to become
part of Wesley's commitment to explore and nurture the intersection
of religion and the creative arts. The gift they made to Wesley's art
endowment almost 20 years ago has made possible this periodic show
highlighting staff, student and faculty work. Their gift encourages
the community to seek a connection between faith and the arts in
perpetuity.

In Wesley's Henry Luce III Center for the Arts and Religion, students
have unique experiences to work with Artists-in-Residence in our
on-campus studio and to explore ways of reaching local communities
and congregations. The dream is kept alive by the dedication and
continuing support of our friends and donors like Jean and Tom.
Tom and Jean have dedicated this exhibition series to the memory of
their daughter Constance.

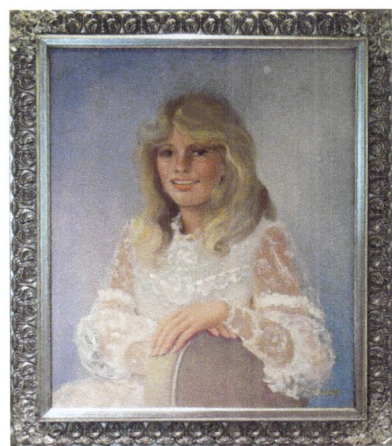

*Portrait of Constance Sherridan
Hefner*

In Memory of
Constance Sherridan Hefner

1997-1998

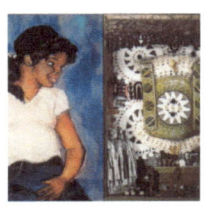

Visions and Memories
Paintings by Barbara Hardaway
and Debra Jean Wilkins-Ambush
July 14 – September 19, 1997

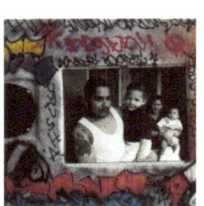

Talking Pictures
Photography and Mixed Media Assemblages
by Roger Marshutz
September 29 – November 7, 1997

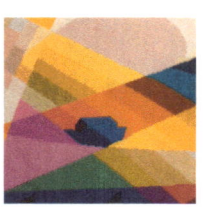

Abiding Presence
A collaborative work designed by Catherine Kapikian
and executed by members of the Church of the Abiding
Presence in Beltsville, MD
November 17, 1997 – January 23, 1998

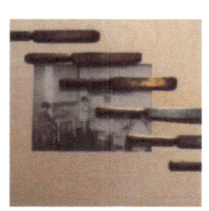

Bread Not Stone
Conceptual artist Barbara Rose Haum
February 3 – March 20, 1998

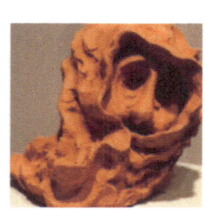

Art in the Seminary: the 3rd Annual WTS Community Show
Works from students, faculty, staff,
and Artists-in-Residence: Christine Parson,
Woong-sik Chon and Momodou Ceesay
April 13 – May 15, 1998

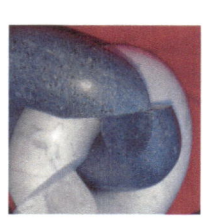

Unite the Pair So Long Disjoined
Sculptures based on mathematics by Helaman Ferguson
May 21 – July 30, 1998

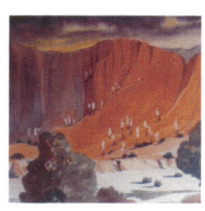

Recent Watercolors
Trever Bennett
June 22 – July 30, 1998
In the Board Room

In reflecting on my 35 year artist/teacher career, I am reminded of the remarkable beginnings of my relationship with the Dadian Gallery at Wesley that has come to influence my decision to recently enter into arts and theological studies at this same institution.

There is transformative work here especially in the areas of urban ministry. This is particularly meaningful to me as I have been able to bring my questions regarding African Americans and their expression of the sacred both historically and contemporarily.

As one of the first two African American women to exhibit at the Wesley Dadian Gallery in 1997, I desired to paint about my own memories of growing up during the 1960s in the Shaw community during the emergent civil rights era. This expression of spiritual and cultural heritage continues to permeate both my writing and artmaking.

The intricate and colorful stained glass windows in Saint Luke's Episcopal Church where I received my baptism as a child remind me that the African American community has always nurtured connections with the sacred through the visual.

When viewing the artist's renderings of the Stations of the Cross at St. Luke's, one recalls great 19th century artists such as Henry Ossawa Tanner whose artistic abilities were cultivated within his church community. We don't celebrate this enough, moreover acknowledge the duality of the mobilizing nature of believing communities in the quest for human dignity.

Recently St. Luke's Episcopal Church hosted five of their youth congregants who attend Duke Ellington Arts High Public School at recital capstone experiences. This kind of collaborative event can be seen as both a curious and encouraging sign regarding the point of intersection between cultural heritage and the worship experience.

As a result of my own exhibition experience at the Dadian Gallery, I anticipate my own writing and artmaking might be emboldened by the blessings of critical inquiry and freedom of artistic expression.

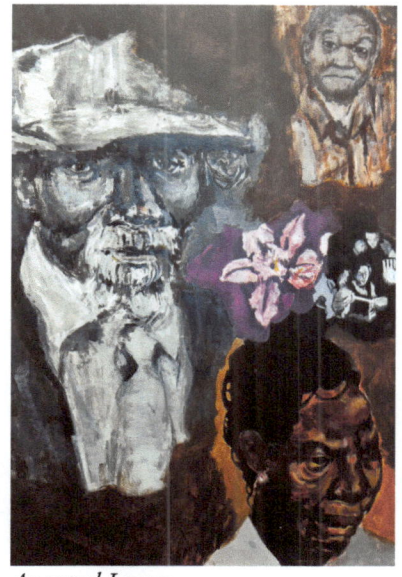

Ancestral Legacy

Debra Jean Wilkins-Ambush
Exhibition 1997

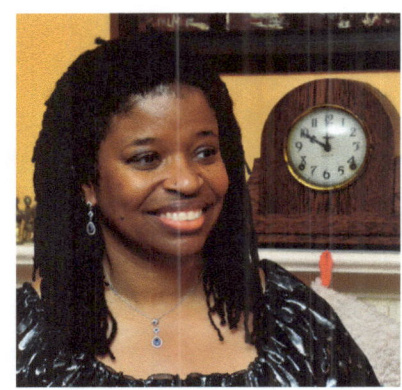

1998-1999

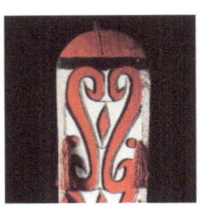

Ancestor War Shields of the Asmat
from the Crosier Collection of
the American Museum of Asmat Art
August 24 – October 9, 1998

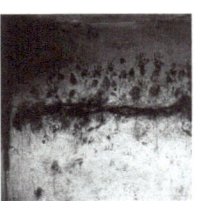

Faith at the Threshold
Photographs by Rose-Lynn Fisher
October 12, 1998 – January 15, 1999

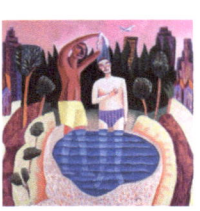

In the Desert
Paintings by James Janknegt
February 15 – March 26, 1999

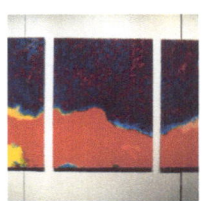

Six Triptychs, Artists and the Holy in the New Millennium
Paintings by Doug Purnell
April 5 – May 14, 1999

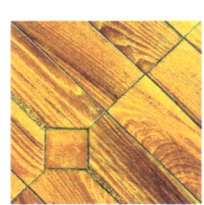

Art in the Seminary:
The 4th Annual WTS Community Show
Students, Staff and Faculty
April 5 – May 14, 1999
In the Board Room

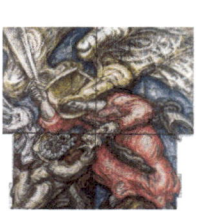

Angel and Prophet
A Gift from the Estate of Alek Rapoport
June 14 – September 17, 1999

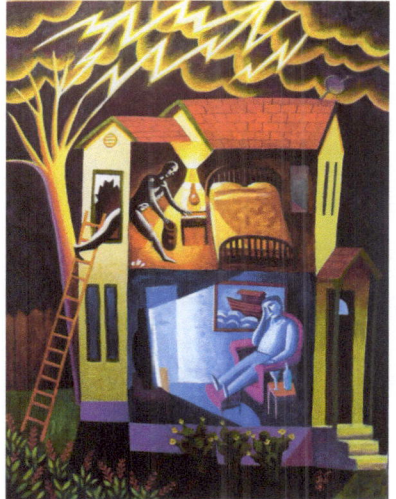

Thief in the Night

James Janknegt
Exhibition 1999

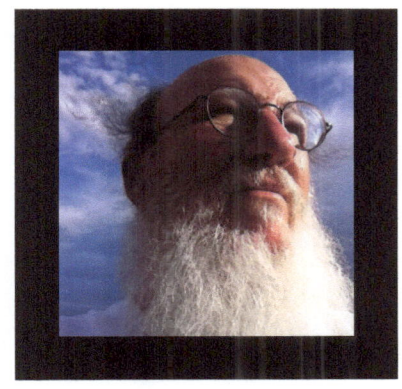

Since I exhibited at the Dadian Gallery in 1999 I began a series of paintings based on the parables of Jesus. So far I have painted around 20 parables. Depending on how you count them there are about 40 parables so I have a ways to go before I get them all done. I hope to publish them once I get them all painted.

My wife and I became Catholics in 2007 and I started a new series of paintings based on the Mysteries of the Rosary. I have painted 20 of these and again, hope to publish these when I am finished. Last year I finished painting the Stations of the Cross and self published a small devotional book.

I have also been busy painting commissions and several murals as well as doing some commercial illustration for a Catholic publishing company.

www.bcartfarm.com

1999-2000

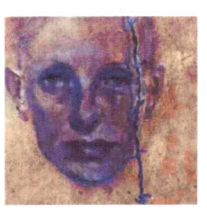

Facing History
Recent Paintings by Judith Peck
September 27 – November 5, 1999

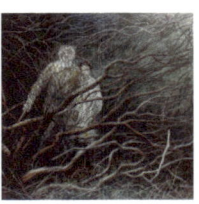

Meditations on Life
Slayton Underhill Retrospective
September 27 – December 10, 1999
In the Board Room

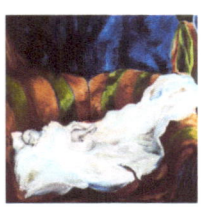

A Record of Baby's Days
A Narrative Installation by Jessica Damen
November 22, 1999 – January 21, 2000

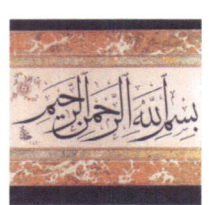

Islamic Calligraphy: A Living Art
Mohamed Zakariya, A. H. Tabnak Rosie White,
and Sylvia Safiyah Godlas
February 7 – March 17, 2000

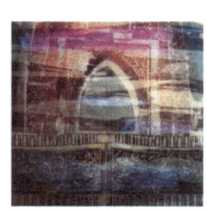

Spiritual Journey Series
Mixed Media by Mansoora Hassan
February 7 – March 17, 2000
In the Board Room

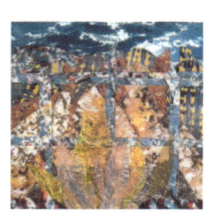

WTS Graduates Exhibition
Works by Graduates of the Seminary
April 3 – May 26, 2000
In the Board Room

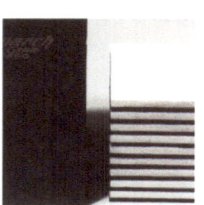

In Process
Paintings and Mixed Media by Eric Shultis
June 12 – July 28, 2000

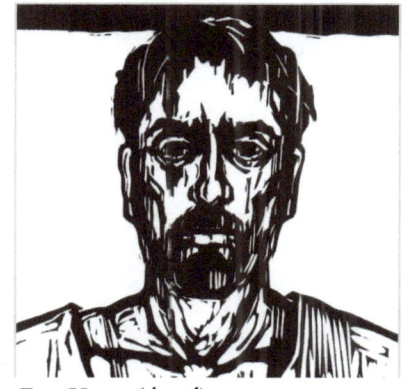

Ecce Homo (detail)

Margaret (Peggy) Adams Parker

Exhibition 2001
Artist-in-Residence
2013 – 2014

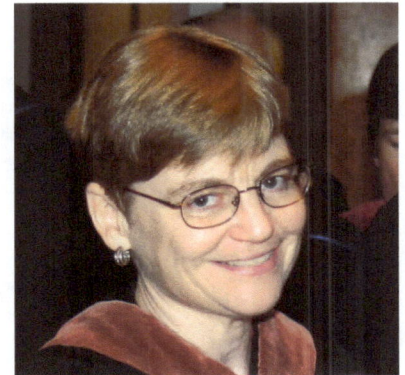

"Esau ran to meet him" was commissioned for *Repair the Future*, a conference convened in Weimar, Germany, to foster reconciliation; the program concluded with a pilgrimage to Buchenwald. The reconciliation of Jacob and Esau seemed an appropriate story to embody the aspirations of *Repair the Future*. It reflected my enduring interest in the power of the visual arts to enlarge our experience of the biblical narrative and my commitment - through my teaching and my art — to the visual arts as a significant "language" in our faith journey. And it manifested my conviction that our gestures tell our life story: the lift of a head or the slump of a shoulder can reveal a person's joy or despair.

I have long admired Wesley's arts programming and, as an adjunct instructor at Virginia Theological Seminary, appreciated the opportunity to work with Cathy Kapikian and Deborah Sokolove through the Washington Theological Consortium. I was consequently grateful for the invitation in 2001 to show my Stations of the Cross at Wesley Seminary. That exhibition served to confirm the significance of the arts in a theological setting. I was likewise pleased to serve last year as Wesley Artist in Residence, working with students to integrate their studio experience and their theological training. I am particularly thankful to my students for their energy and insight, and I hope that they discover ways to integrate what they have experienced in the studio into their future ministries.

www.margaretadamsparker.com

2000-2001

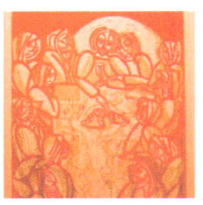

The Artist and the Bible: 20th Century Works on Paper
From the Collection of Edward and Diane Knippers
August 28 – October 6, 2000

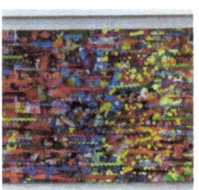

Net and Other Narratives
An Installation by Kevin Harris
October 16 – November 24, 2000

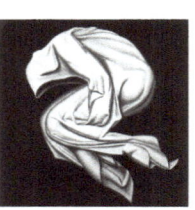

Mysteries and Meditations
Paintings by Ted Kliman
December 11, 2000 – February 9, 2001

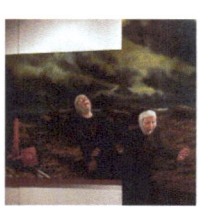

Tenebrae
Paintings by Melissa Weinman
February 19 – April 6, 2001

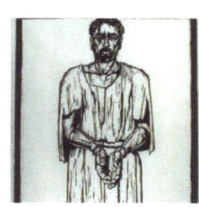

"Then they led him out to crucify him."
Stations of the Cross and Other Woodcuts
by Margaret Adams Parker
February 19 – April 6, 2001
In the Board Room

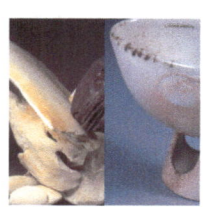

Conversations
Ceramics by Joyce Michaud and Ray Chen
April 16 – June 8, 2001

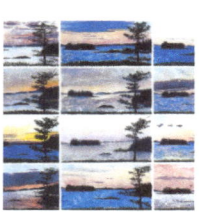

Atmospheric Transitions
Paintings by Mary Prince
An Exhibition in Honor of Trever Bennett
June 25 – August 3, 2001

In Memoriam

It was not long after my father draped his tallit over a manikin for the first time that he began to glimpse the possibilities before him.

He bent the manikin forward, and, fascinated by the way the cloth stretched taut across its back, sought to capture what he saw. Bent it back, and drew the way it sagged, the limp and shadowed dip. He splayed its arms, and drew that. Splayed its arms and legs, and drew that. Bent it forward from the waist, stretching it into positions that would have caused an actual person intense, shooting pain, and drew that. Scissored its arms and legs into a soaring arabesque, and drew that.

Now he began combining positions, bending and splaying, stretching and scissoring. With each change of position, the cloth itself seemed to change, and necessitated a new way of expressing that movement on paper or canvas.

Eventually he discovered that he did not need to subject the poor manikin to abuse, that he understood the way the fabric responded to the movements of the body well enough that he could invent.

And once he was able to invent, he was able to move from drawing to painting, in other words, to translating the image before him into something more luminous, mysterious, and heightened than (mere) reality.

He had grown frustrated with the clever, facile art he had been making for the past decade, paintings that were empty of meaning for him. He worked, now, toward the opposite goal. Not to provoke thought, as most of his contemporaries wanted for their art, but to speak simply and elicit emotion.

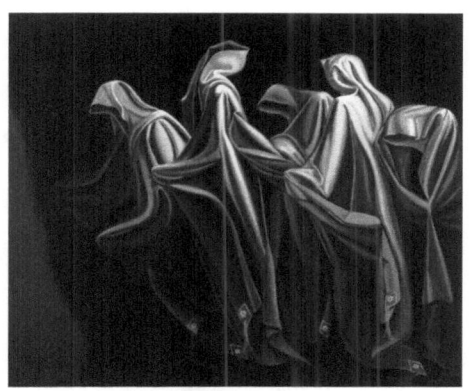

The Dance of Death

Ted Kliman
(1929 – 2009)
Exhibition 2001
Artist-in-Residence
2000 – 2001

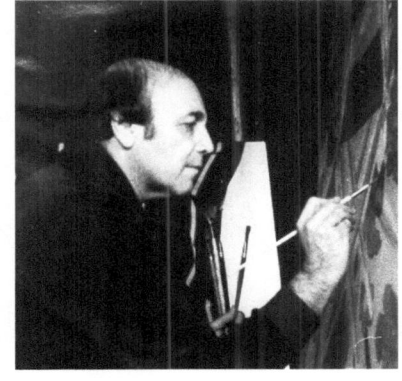

The surrealists had been an early inspiration. He had drawn heavily from figure painters like Philip Pearlstein. He owed a debt to the artists of the Color School and their use of large, abstracted planes of bold and vivid paint. But now he simplified his palette and leaned on the lessons of the old masters.

A mourning figure, in the manner of Mary Magdalene. An annunciation, arms lifted toward the heavens. A crucifix.

Why so few Jewish artists had made use of this rich tradition was a mystery to him. Was the Jew meant to think "Christian" when he gazed up at the soaring, twisting bodies of el Greco and Caravaggio — bathed in bands of light and dark, sometimes tortured, sometimes ecstatic?

Their canvases often depicted Christ and other figures of the New Testament, yes, but they transcended this context, too; transcended the commissions of popes and bishops and cardinals. The paintings, specific in their visceral tactility, were universal in their exploration of the experience of being alive, of the pain and suffering that are inescapable, and the pursuit of beauty and exaltation that bring, to us, the earthbound, a measure of grace and redemption.

Todd Kliman

2001-2002

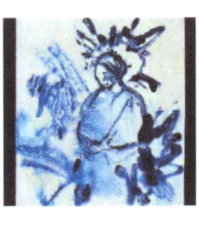

The Visible Word:
Works by Past and Present Artists-in-Residence
Avignon, Brophy, Caughy, Ellis, Hardaway, Lan, McCollough,
Montgomery, Nankervis, Parson, Pierce, Sokolove, Xenakis, Yu
August 27 – October 5, 2001

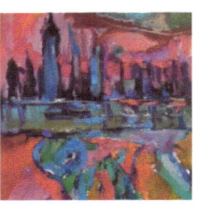

New York Kaddish
Paintings by Toni Franovic
September 25 – December 18, 2001
In the Board Room

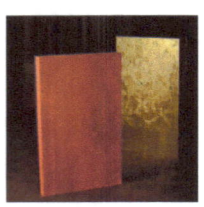

Recent Works
Works by Makoto Fujimura
October 22, 2001 – January 7, 2002

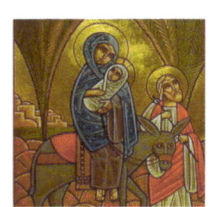

Window into Eternity: A Rediscovery of Holy Images
A Traveling Exhibition
from Christians in the Visual Arts (CIVA)
January 18 – March 1, 2002

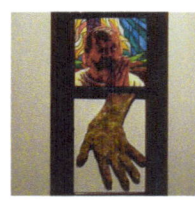

A Circle of Twelve: Recent Paintings/Assemblages
by Tim Timmerman
March 18 – May 17, 2002

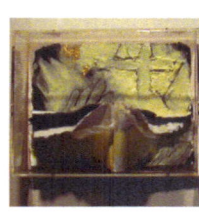

Healing: a Personal Journey
Paintings by Carolyn Manosevitz
May 28 – August 2, 2002

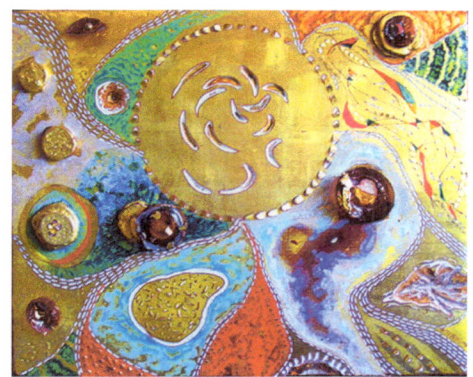
When the Ice Melts

Thomas Xenakis
Exhibitions 2005 & 2009
Artist-in-Residence 1996

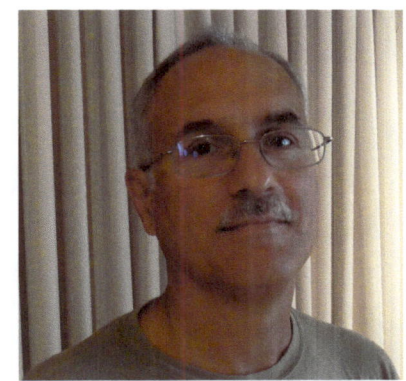

For many years my concentration as a visual artist has been to bring the realms of sacred and secular art together. My impetus is derived from my Eastern Orthodox Christian faith and its aesthetic legacy in Scripture, Church tradition, history, and the arts. My training and practice in hagiography (icon writing) and in secular painting have fueled and synthesized my creative vision.

My ongoing contemporary series titled: XPYSO (meaning "gold" in the Greek language) is inspired by the defaced and scarred surfaces of Medieval Byzantine iconographic imagery. These panels are prepared in the traditional methods and materials of icon painting. Art panels serve as corpus and various kinds of marks on the ground of the work represent variables of modern life. These works visually address the search for God, our selves, and our planet in a quest for beauty, oneness, and wholeness.

My work on these gilded panels includes color, textures, patterns and movements. These gilded panels reveal the nature of light. The gold symbolic of divinity and enlightenment, as it is real, inner, and reflected light. The random marks, whether painted, chiseled, punched, adhered, or incised, are symbolic of our humanity.

My hope in bridging the sacred and the secular are communicated in this divine/human duality inherent in Christianity, but also in other faith journeys. Abstracted imagery, whether in the Holy iconographic image or in the secular panels, expresses a variety of themes. Subjects from Scripture, Holy personages, liturgy, creation, ecology, current events are evident in this series. Imagery is biological, cellular, organic, topographic, and cosmic in form and space. Dialogue through this art shares an ultimate goal of theosis, unification with God.

www.xenakisarts.com

2002-2003

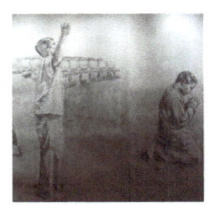

A Glimpse into the Christian Mind
Drawings by Melissa Ignatuk
August 26 – October 20, 2002

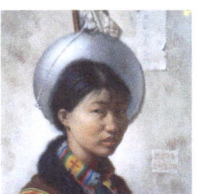

Portraits of China
Paintings by Gerhardt Miller
September 3 – November 4, 2002
In the Board Room

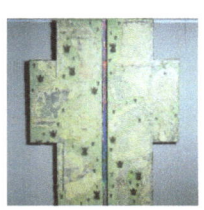

Cross Sections
Mixed Media Assemblages by Robert Peppers
October 28 – December 18, 2002

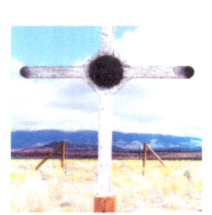

Grave Images, A Faith Visualized
Artist's Books by Kathy Hettinga
January 21 – March 14, 2003

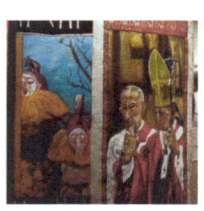

Moving Towards Center
Paintings by Sharlene Packer
March 28 – May 23, 2003

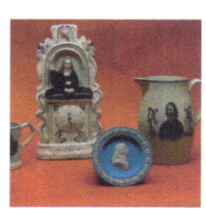

Remembering John Wesley
Celebrating the 300th Anniversary of his Birth from the
Collections of the United Methodist Archive and History
Center at Drew University. Guest Curator, Kenneth Rowe
June 2 – July 25, 2003

My first experience of the Dadian Gallery was an invitation in 2003 to exhibit my work, *Grave Images: A Faith Visualized*. The artwork looked fabulous in the space. I gave an artist's talk and Deborah Sokolove, then Curator, now Director of the Center, wrote beautifully about my art for the brochure and website. Deborah and I had first met in the early 90s as colleagues in the then-new field of computer art. Several years later, I received the Artist-in-Residence and spent the spring of 2009 at the Henry Luce III Center for the Arts and Religion. My time was filled with teaching diverse seminarians the art of putting text and image together to make books, taking three courses for credit—ranging from the New Testament Epistles to the Holy in D.C., making art in the studio with Distinguished Artist-in-Residence—Catherine Kapikian, exhibiting my work in the Dadian Gallery, showing my students' artists' books in the chapel narthex, singing in the chapel choir, and conversing with faculty, seminarians, and visiting artists and scholars. Being a part of the intellectual and creative life of the seminary was a rich experience and profound blessing.

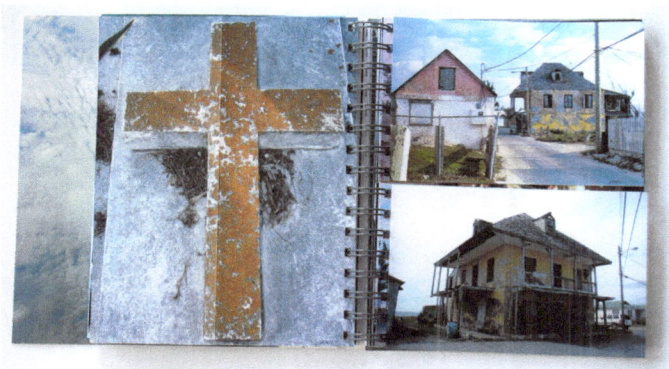

Bahama Book

Kathy T. Hettinga
Exhibition 2003
Artist-in-Residence 2009

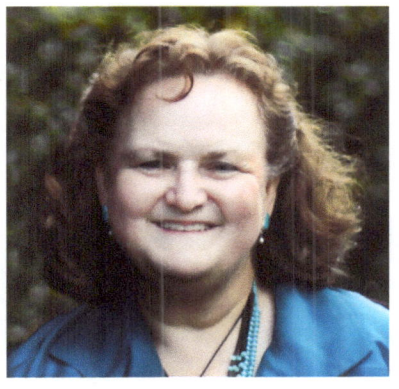

The intersection of art and faith has always been my passion. I feel at home while working and studying at seminaries. Theological study is relevant to artists. The arts are relevant to theological institutions. Christianity, religion, theology and faith address questions of creation, meaning, purpose, suffering, sin, and death. The great questions of life are often best addressed in the creative, visual, embodied language of art. While Artist-in-Residence at The Center for Arts and Religion I found the time and space to work on a large design project for an activist cause, *Middle East Baltimore Stories, Images and Words from a Displaced Community*, and I finished the intense editing process of my book, *Grave Images: The San Luis Valley, Colorado*, which was published in 2009 by the Museum of New Mexico Press.

The Grave Images project began when I decided to photograph all of the cemeteries in the San Luis Valley—burial plots, private and public, Pentecostal, Penitente, Protestant and Catholic—to explain to myself and to others the mysteries of death, and faithful hope. I found a shared sorrow in the grave images in the cemeteries, and I was comforted. Through photographing cemeteries around the world—in Azerbaijan, Russia, Colombia, Australia, and the islands of the Bahamas—I have seen the creative human response to our greatest enemy, death. I then sought to offer comfort to others through my art—photographs, digital prints, and artist's books. These artworks come alongside the viewer and weep with them, and travel to places I will never go. The Holy Spirit speaks through these works to viewers I will never meet.

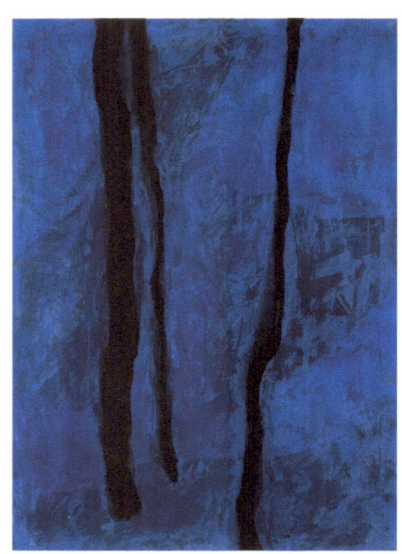

Black on Ultramarine

Douglas Purnell

Exhibition 1999
Artist-in-Residence
1994, 1998 & 2009

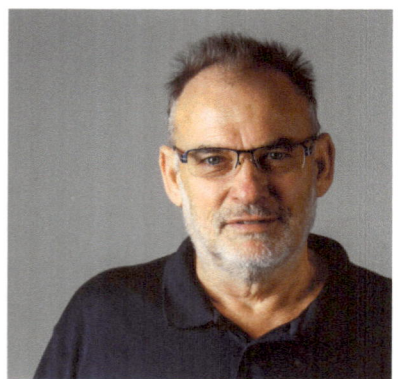

I have been richly blessed to be an artist/scholar in residence at the Henry Luce III Center for the Arts and Religion at Wesley Seminary three times. How have these times shaped me as artist and as theologian? Firstly, as a minister in a parish, and later as a faculty member, here in Australia to be welcomed into the seminary community and to have a time and space to work with discipline in an appreciative and professionally critical community has been very important in my ongoing professional development as minister, as artist, as pastoral theologian and as author.

Before I came to CAR the first time I had just completed a doctorate "Doing theology through expressive art: a series of paintings informed by the theology of Paul Tillich" in which I painted a series of non objective abstract paintings which were hung in the worship space, and I listened for how they influenced people's worship. When I returned in 1998 I had met and been influenced by the work of Friedhelm Mennekes, a German Jesuit Pastoral Theologian who, at St Peter's in Cologne, had removed all of the "kitsch Catholic" material from the church and invited major world artists to create triptychs which would be placed in St Peters for two months. This work is documented in the book *Tryptychon*. Before coming to the CAR again, I sat in my local church at worship, and imagined a triptych there. That became the focus of my work while in Washington. I produced 7 triptychs which might be used in a worship space. That work was shown in the Dadian Gallery. My only disappointment was that I couldn't visit to see the exhibition.

My own art practice has been significantly shaped by my visits to CAR. Meeting and relating with Cathy Kapikian has been special in so many ways, and I have valued her willingness to comment on my continuing art practice. I have quite a number of her responses pinned to my studio walls. In 2011 I retired from full time ministry with a goal of working full time in my studio for the next 15 years. I am doing that and enjoying the way in which my work changes and grows as I work at it every day.

I want to make paintings that are substantial, profound and true. I want to make paintings that have a purpose, a reason, and that are authentic. I want to make paintings invite spirit and mystery to dwell. I am working on two themes … the first is the face and the second the land. I want to sing to the surface of both face and land, the mystery that slumbers beneath the surface. In a busy, noisy, world I want to encourage people to be open to being addressed by the mystery that is beyond speech.

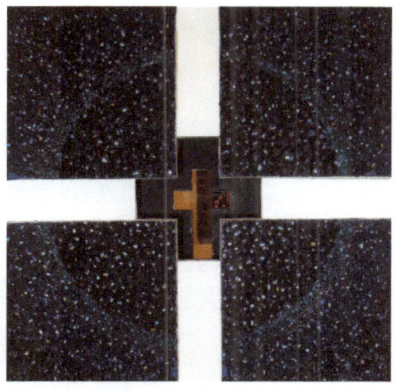

Dark Matters Greek Cross

Robert E. Peppers
Exhibition 2002
Artist-in-Residence
2007 – 2008

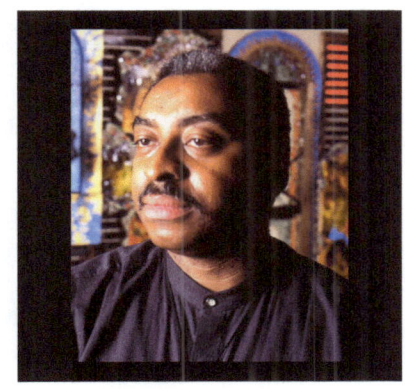

I have served as an Artist-in-Residence from September of 2007 through May of 2008 at the Henry Luce III Center for the Arts and Religion, Wesley Theological Seminary, in Washington D.C. During that time, I created the "Gifts," a twelve piece mixed media series. The title "Gifts" refers to the life sustaining elements found in nature such as Earth, Air, Water, Fire and Space.

The series consists of geometric shapes arranged on the wall to resemble a display of gift box lids. Each work represents a precious gift to mankind. Its sections are arranged around a particular prayer symbol. Conceptually, ribbons are replaced by negative cross-space, "perfect absence." The "cross voided" or hole in a work is designed to convey the perception of space as spiritually replete.

A Reflection…

While on a coffee break outside Kresge's Art Studio, I was grappling with what other gift to explore after the completion of works representing the Five Great Elements. Suddenly, a magnolia cone fell with a thump on the picnic table spilling my coffee. I examined its elegant scales and pale waxy surface. Then, I pried it open to reveal a bright little red seed inside. Thus, "Seeds" became the next "Gift" in the series. It was literally a "gift" of inspiration from above (smile.)

"Seeds" features a dismembered cross cut in five pieces inset in four corner sections. The center contains a hole in a square of rich brown soil. This is symbolic of the crucial point for germinating a single red seed from those that compose the cross arms and upright. Coincidentally, the Maha bindu, is known as "the great seed point" of the Sri Yantra meditation diagram. Subsequently, magnolia cone scales in the corner sections are transposed into a field of budding sprouts painted in sunshine yellow, spring green and raindrop blue.

2003-2004

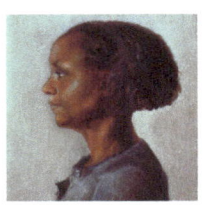

Hand and Eye: Artists-in-Residence 2002-2004
Constance Sherridan Hefner Memorial Exhibition
Sally Avignone, Sarah Demas, Jeffery Lewis, Hal Malone,
Lilya, Sue Mink, Jiha Moon, and Judy Shapiro
August 25 – October 10, 2003

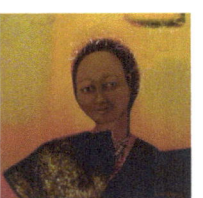

Visions and Voices:
Embroidered Textiles from Honduras, Mexico and Uganda
From the collection of Brenda Kingery
October 20 – December 12, 2003

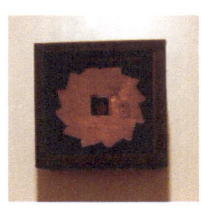

States of Grace
Sculptures by Margo Klass
Prose poems by Frank Soos
January 12 – March 12, 2004

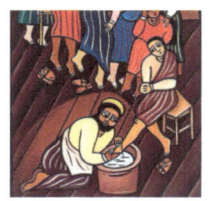

The Book of the Gospels and Other Work
Paintings by Laura James
January 12 – March 12, 2004
In the Board Room

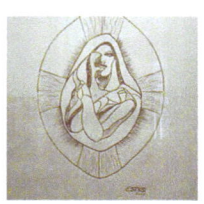

The Seminary Celebrates:
Recent Works by Students, Staff and Faculty
March 29 – May 14, 2004

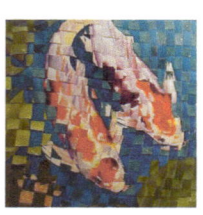

The Watercolors
by Carroll Saussy
March 29 – May 14, 2004
In the Board Room

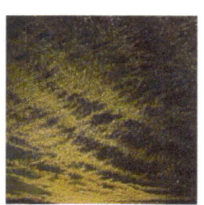

Towards Ontario
Encaustic Paintings by Jeffrey Lewis
An Exhibition in Honor of Trever Bennett
June 1 – July 30, 2004

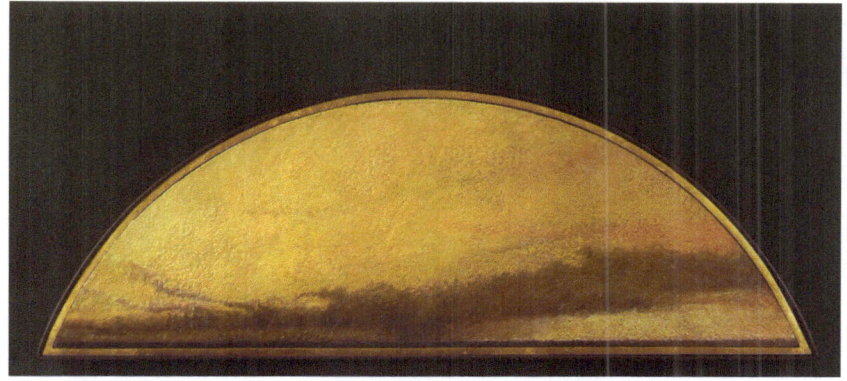

Squall

Living among a community of writers, dancers, divinity students and seekers during my stay as an Artist-In-Residence at Wesley, a shared vision of proclaiming God's redeeming work in His creation was the focus of our daily discipline. Upon entering the visual arts studio one could see, neatly printed in white chalk on a board suspended from the studio's wall the phrase, "The workshop hums, and the honey reeks of thyme." A singular sentence from Virgil's poem describing the life of the bee, and an apt description of our daily task within the studio; the slow, steady undertaking to realize a gradually developing image or series of images that throughout its sometimes-painful birthing would eventually give voice to that inclination that prompted it. While the studio functioned as the workshop of labor for the artist, the gallery serves as the place where the fruits of those labors can be seen. Here, the veracity of one's efforts is exposed, examined, discussed, contemplated and (for the artist/maker, constantly questioned). It is also here, in a space like the Dadian Gallery, that the artist/maker is given the opportunity to acknowledge the gift of being presented a forum in which to express his/her efforts and, therefore, to become a participant in redemption's dialogue. For the artist, this is a very great Gift, indeed.

Jeffrey Lewis
Exhibition 2004
Artist-in-Residence
2003 – 2004

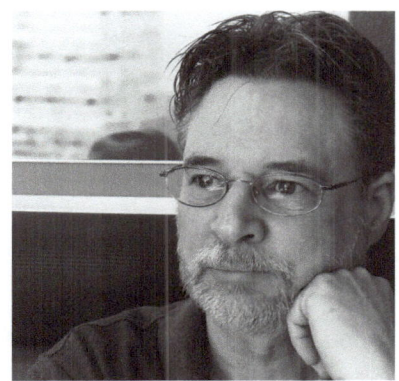

2004-2005

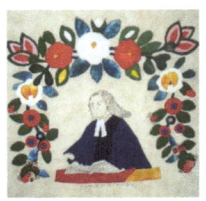

The John Wesley Baltimore Album Quilt
Guest Curator, Judy Shapiro
August 30 — September 17, 2004

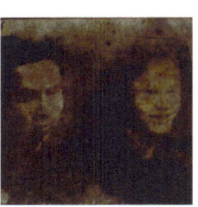

A Story to be Told
Prints by Pauline Jakobsberg
September 27 — October 22, 2004
In the Board Room

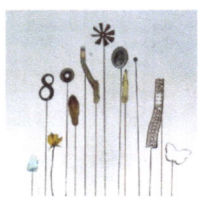

The Square Halo
Constructions and Collages by John Sager
November 1 — December 17, 2004

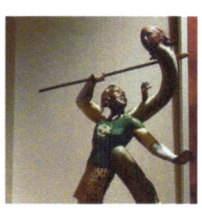

Artists-in-Residence 2004-2005:
Patrick Michael Birge, Marie Pavlicek-Wehrli,
and Yoshiko Oishi (Meiran)
November 1 — December 17, 2004
In the Board Room

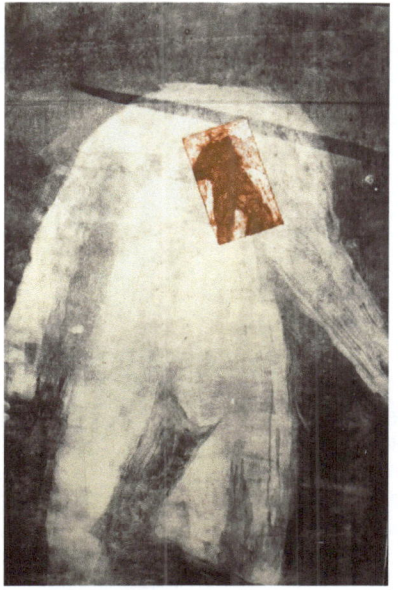

A Mere Shadow

Pauline Jakobsberg
Exhibition 2004

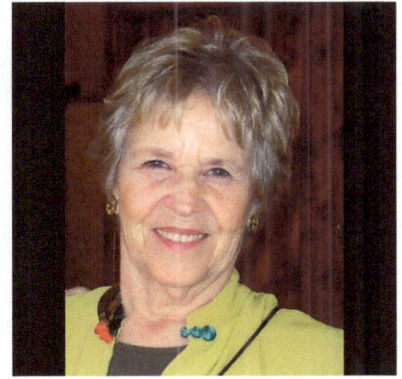

The driving force behind my artwork was inspired by my late husband's family who were Holocaust survivors as well as my own American roots, memory drawings, journals and found objects. Exhibiting at the Dadian Gallery gave me the opportunity to share my visual stories in an incredible atmosphere of spirituality and faith. I recall a quiet chamber with inner movable walls creating an almost theater in the round; a feeling of a place to rest. My husband helped me bring the work to the gallery and unfortunately two days before the reception, he passed away. Prior to the closing of my exhibit I returned to absorb these peaceful surroundings during a very difficult period in my life. I continue making art and sharing his stories. This coming October, 2014, I will be exhibiting at the Houston Holocaust Museum.

continued

2004-2005

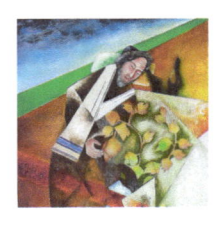
The Hebrew Bible and the Arts
Members of the Doctor of Ministry Track in Art and Theology
January 5 – March 4, 2005
In the Board Room

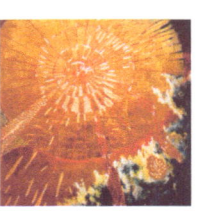
XPYSO (GOLD)
Paintings by Thomas Xenakis
January 18 – March 4, 2005

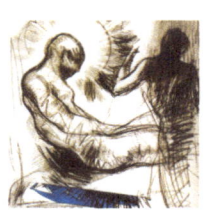
Bearing Witness:
Lamentations of War and other Works on Paper
by Constance Pierce
March 14 – April 4, 2005
In the Board Room

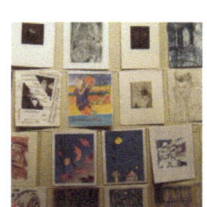
September 11 Memorial Portfolio
The American Print Alliance
March 14 – April 4, 2005

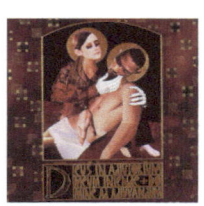
Pages from Prayer Books
Mixed Media by Jan Richardson
April 11 – May 27, 2005

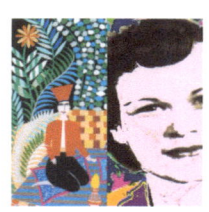
Memory and Story
Paintings and Mixed Media
by Ellouise Schoettler and Helen Zughaib
June 13 – July 29, 2005

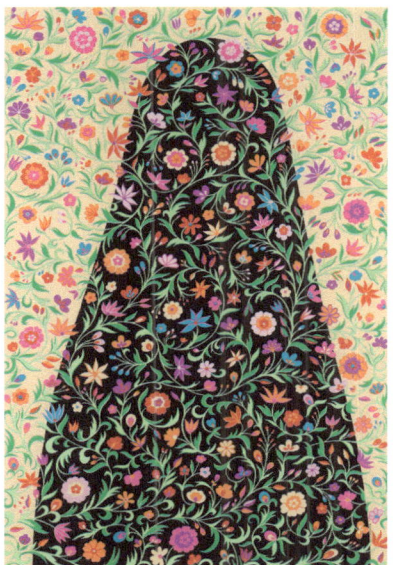

Arab Spring

Helen Zughaib
Exhibition 2005

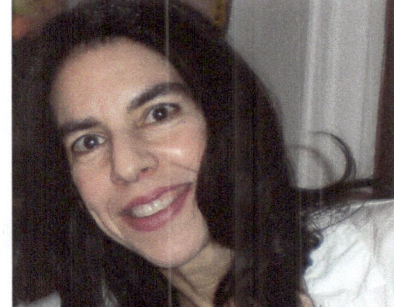

Since March 2011, I have been working on pieces with regards to the "Arab Spring," that ultimately began with Mohamed Bouazizi, the Tunisian fruit seller, who set himself on fire in front of the government buildings to protest his harsh treatment at the hands of government officials. The protests and demonstrations that ensued and spread all over the Arab world, began with high hopes and optimism never before seen. With those first heady and exuberant months, I painted my first piece "Arab Spring 1" to reflect the contagious optimism that spread globally and specifically to Arab American communities worldwide.

As time passed however, revolutions and street protests turned into bloody battles and has since resulted in the current tragic civil war in Syria. And my work on the Arab Spring began also to reflect those changing emotions and dynamics of the initial optimism.
In my fist painting "Arab Spring 1," I used the flower motif to denote the powerful feeling of hope and renewal, a rebirth if you will. I continued to use that flower motif in much of the subsequent pieces devoted to my Spring series. I have also used words, both in English and in Arabic, and in several pieces restrict my palette to black and white for further emotional emphasis. I also have created work that specifically addresses female issues within the context of the Arab Spring.

Despite the incredible sadness, loss of life and displacement of thousands, I do keep my hopes and prayers for an Arab world that is peaceful, democratic and free, and respects the rights of each of its citizens.

www.hzughaib.com

2005-2006

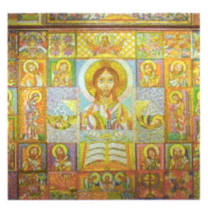

Dreaming of Judgment Day:
Paintings by Boris Kozlov (1937-1999)
August 22 – October 7, 2005

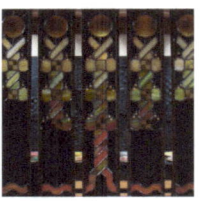

Mysterium Fidei
An Installation by Patrick Ellis and Friends
October 24 – December 16, 2005

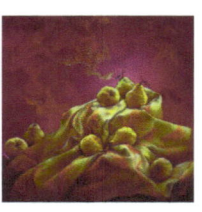

2005 Artists-in-Residence Recent Works
Shirah Rachel Apple, Heidi Christensen,
Sarah Demas, and Rod Jellema
November 21 – December 16, 2005
In the Board Room

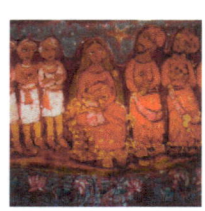

Seeing with Indian Eyes
The Art and Faith of P. Solomon Raj
January 17 – March 3, 2006

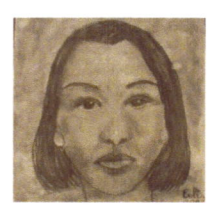

The Seminary Celebrates...Again!
Recent Works by Students, Staff, and Faculty
March 20 – May 12, 2006

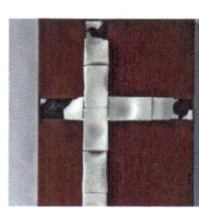

The Reconstituted Cross
Sculpture by Theodore Prescott
June 1 – July 28, 2006

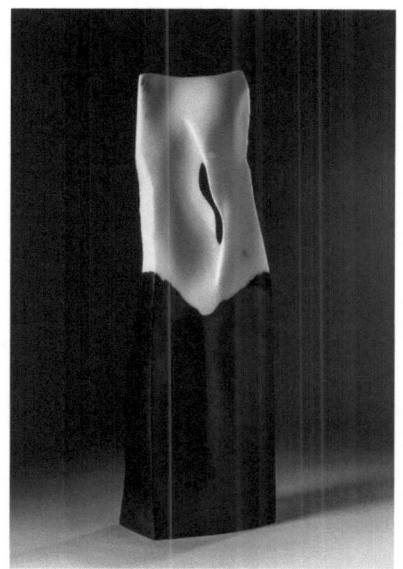

Small Stele (Wound)

Theodore Prescott
Exhibition 2006

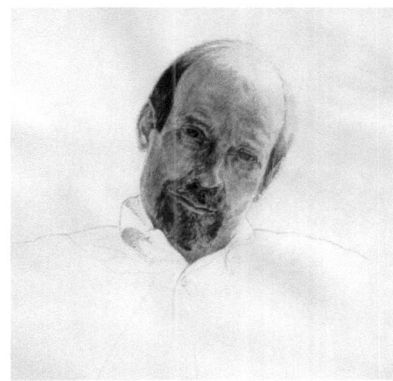

Drawing by Catherine Prescott

I exhibited at the Dadian Gallery in the summer of 2006. Since it is a gallery connected to a seminary, I chose to display a series of crosses I'd begun making in the early 1980's. I titled the exhibit *The Reconstituted Cross*. My goal throughout the series was to reimagine and reenergize a visual cliché. I wanted crosses that could be experienced for their art. That seemed practical and achievable, given the prominence of the cross in art's history.

The exhibit gave me a chance to see the evolution of my work in one repeated subject. It became obvious to me that my interest in the substance of art had grown over time. I like what the unique properties of a material bring to an image's metaphorical allusions. This was especially evident in a salt lick cross in the Dadian exhibit, where the cross was formed though cows licking salt blocks. That cross has been popular, and I've made several variations of it over the years.

The work in this exhibit, "Small Stele (Wound)," continues my interest in imagery that is mediated by the nature of substances. In its case, an apparently opaque solid is revealed to be translucent when carved "thin." Light imagery is a hidden possibility within some marbles. I think of the piece here as a model for a larger stele, the vertical slabs which have been used throughout history for commemorative purposes.

www.tedprescottsculpture.com

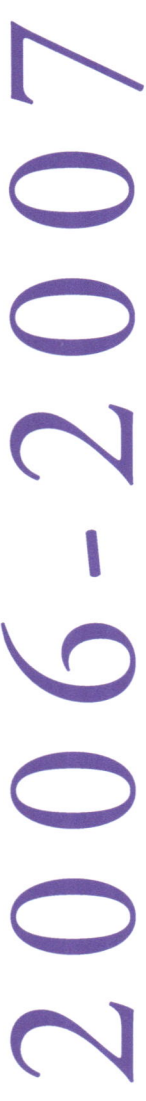

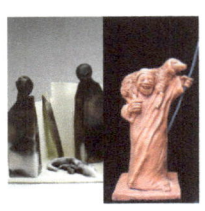

Clay Bodies
by Charles McCollough and Rosemarie Schiller
August 28 – October 6, 2006

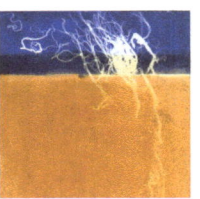

Seeing God: A Visual Exploration of the Spiritual
The Washington Printmakers Gallery and the Dadian Gallery
October 23 – December 15, 2006

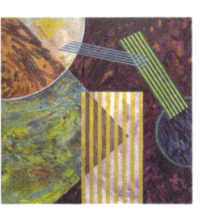

A Visiting Artist Returns
Paintings by Abner Hershberger
An Exhibition in Honor of Trever Bennett
January 16 – March 9, 2007

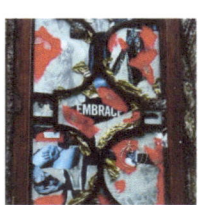

Through the Window: Insight on the Spirituality of AIDS
Lois Wilson
January 16 – March 9, 2007
In the Board Room

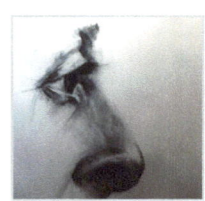

Fresh from the Studio: Artists-in-Residence 2006-2007
Heidi Christensen, Sarah Demas, Nina Falk,
David Kamm, and Iveta Kosyan
March 19 – May 11, 2007

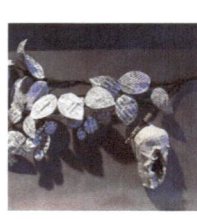

Speaking Volumes: Transforming Hate
Students Working with David Kamm
March 19 – May 11, 2007
In the Board Room

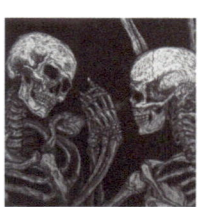

Critical Mass
Etchings & Woodcuts by Trudi Y. Ludwig
June 4 – July 20, 2007

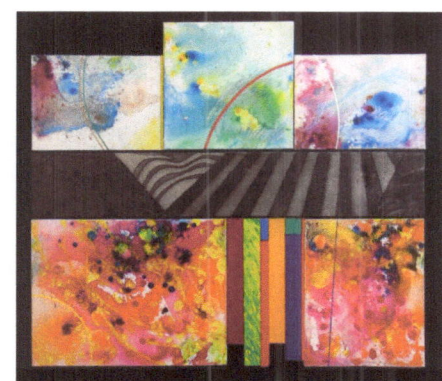

Heritage Field as Color I
from the collection of James Stemen

Abner Hershberger

Exhibition 2007
Artist-in-Residence
1981 – 1982

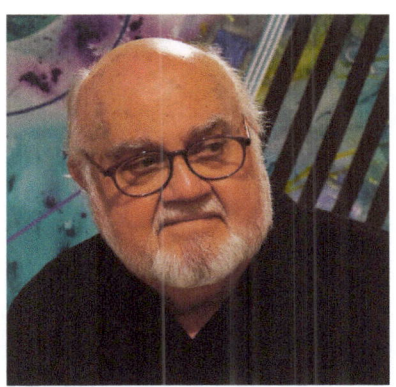

Prior to serving as the first Artist-in-Residence at Wesley Theological Seminary in 1981-82, my art reflected images of the mid-west flatland—vast expanses of expressive grids of grain punctuated with cultivation. These were fields I plowed well into adulthood. The stark markings of furrowed land, patterns of irrigation, and stubble fields seemed almost poetic, and thus became a constant source of material for visual expression.

At Wesley, interaction with students and faculty prompted many thoughtful discussions on how art and faith influence each other. The abstracted fields found in my paintings became personal, spiritual explorations.

Twenty-five years later, in 2007, I had an opportunity to have a solo exhibit at the Dadian Gallery. It was apparent that the serendipitous treatment of the field forms were more colorful, consolidated, and complex. I often observe artists, when responding to religious organizations sponsoring art exhibitions, struggling to stay inside the boundaries of personal expression that carries the "right" literal message. I never hear or see jazz musicians being concerned about that. They know deep-down that a spiritual chord is struck when creative and profound instrumentation is achieved, when the sound is "right."

Currently, that feeling of the jazz musician is what I experience when color and form express what words never can accomplish. Nothing more need be asked of the visual artist who works in an abstract aesthetic.

www.abnerhershberger.com

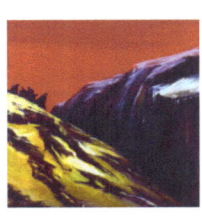

Uprooted
Paintings by Lucy Janjigian
August 27 — October 5, 2007

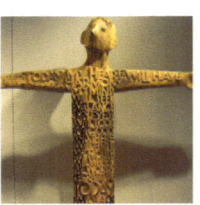

Body of Christ
A Juried Exhibition Sponsored by
the Washington Theological Consortium
October 29 — December 14, 2007

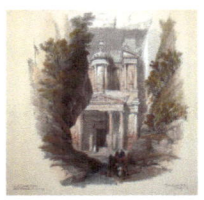

The Holy Land and Egypt through 19th Century Eyes
Lithography by David Roberts
January 24 — March 7, 2008

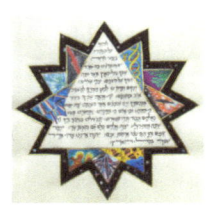

I Will Wake the Dawn: Illuminated Psalms
Paintings by Debra Band
January 24 — March 7, 2008
In the Board Room

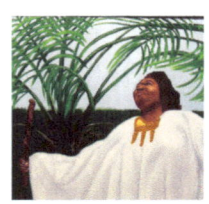

The Seminary Celebrates 2008:
An Exhibition in Honor of Constance Sherridan Hefner
Works by Students, Staff, and Faculty
March 24 — May 16, 2008

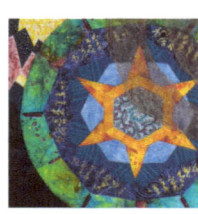

Recent Quilts
by Margreta Silverstone
May 27 — July 25, 2008

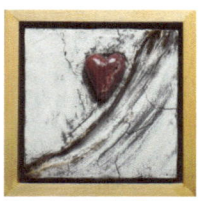

Stations of the Cross: the Weight of Dust
by Kathryn Cramer Brown
May 27 — July 25, 2008
In Oxam Chapel

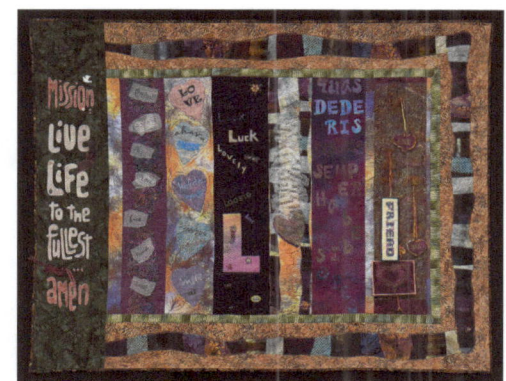

Sacred Words

Margreta Silverstone
Exhibition 2008

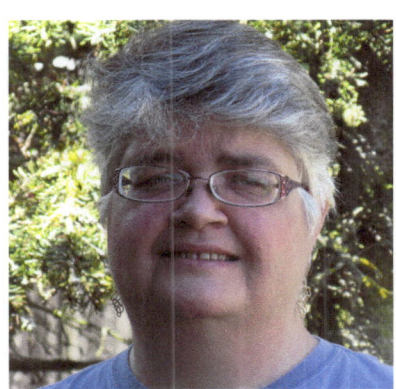

I was part of the Dadian Gallery in 2008. Because other aspects of my life have changed, I have not done as much public display of my work.

I value the creative process. I value the integration of a familiar medium (quilting) into a different avenue of expression. I value the patterns and colors that traditional quilt designs provide. The roots of traditional quilting can still be seen in my work. And I value the connections that being rooted in that tradition gives me and to so many within various faith communities. I value the conversations that have taken place which often unfold with opening comments such as "Wow, my [mom, aunt, grandmother] used to…"

As a person who has also spent time in the computer industry, my patterning has become more complicated, the layers more involved and my work has included other materials. My art is not meant for your bed. And, my art continues to inform my faith and my understanding of my place in this world. Practically speaking, that has meant paying attention to the beauty of God's world around me, staying grounded in my environment, caring for those around me through my work.

Certainly, I was and continue to be grateful for the validation that I found along the way for my work as an artist.

www.margreta.com

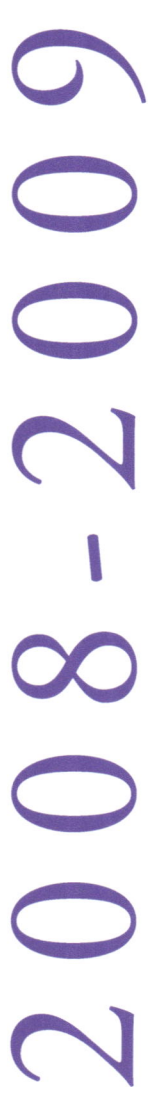

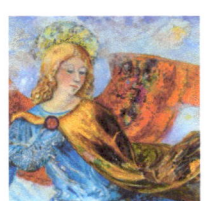

Angels: A Celestial Visitation
Paintings by Patricia M. Friend
August 25 – October 3, 2008

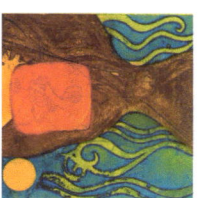

Visual Exegesis:
Religious Images by African American Artists
from the Jean and Robert E. Steele Collection
October 13 – December 12, 2008

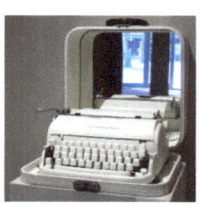

Art+Text: Images, Concepts and Insghts
A Group Exhibition from CIVA (Christians in the Visual Arts)
January 22 – March 4, 2009

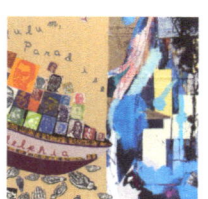

From the Studio: Artists-in-Residence 2007-2009
Kip Deeds, Kumar Duppati, Cynthia Greene, Jennifer Lea
Hall, Kathy Hettinga, Tim Holmes, Sudhir Kim Jackson,
Robert Peppers, Karen Schiff, and James Quentin Young
March 16 – May 15, 2009

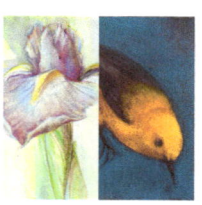

Out of the Land
by Heidi Christensen and Stephen Estrada
An Exhibition in Memory of Trever Bennet
June 1 – July 31, 2009

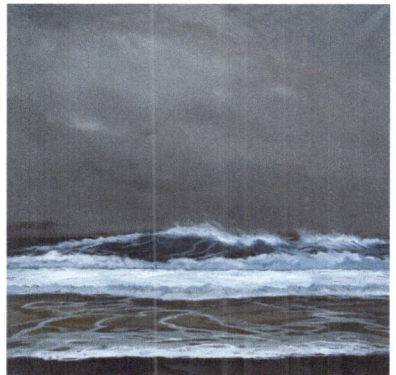

Half Moon Bay

Stephen Estrada
Exhibition 2009

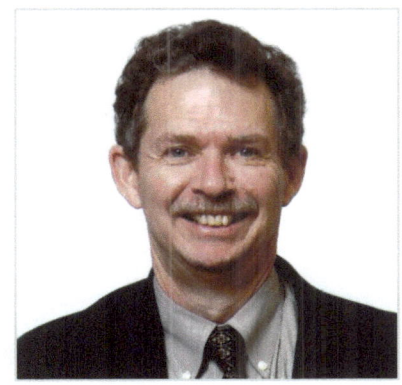

Following several trips to my home waters along the Pacific and to the Gulf Coast where my daughters and I have helped rebuild houses following hurricane Katrina, my artistic focus gravitated towards the sea and the natural environment. I grew up in southern California where I spent many hours in the cold Pacific Ocean creating an early appreciation for the immense power of the sea. Such experiences have resulted in renderings of nature not as an idyllic postcard but a beautiful yet turbulent force. Each painting derives from a journey and a place in my experience. They are not a travelogue but a reminder of our dwelling spot at the slender edge of the elements.

Painting from nature is for me a spiritual and emotional journey. Time, light and place are the critical elements. Just as the waves in some of these paintings are shaped by unseen bathymetric forms, unconscious forces also shape our lives to create form, substance and meaning. Painting is for me an active meditation on the places I seek out: the coordinates where land, sea and air come together, when the light is changing and seemingly stable terra firma is transformed.

These paintings have a cumulative effect on audiences. While each painting may be viewed as representing a moment in place and time, shown together they evoke strong sensory and emotional responses in people. One viewer remarked, "these paintings are not about the land or sea but about how you feel when you are with them."

www.stephenestradaart.com

2009-2010

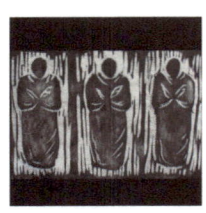

An Artist's Reaction to War
War Memorial: Iraq and Afghanistan
A Group Exhibition with Guest Curator Cecilia Rossey
August 31 – October 9, 2009

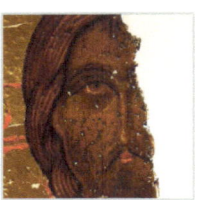

Icons in the American Style
by Peter Pearson and Thomas Xenakis
October 28 – December 18, 2009

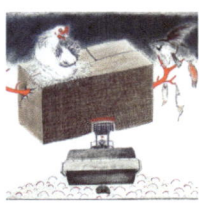

Rosemary Luckett: Paradise in the Balance
Mixed Media Drawings and Collage
January 22 – March 12, 2010

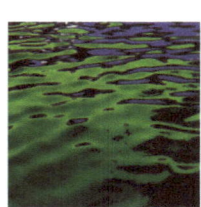

The Seminary Celebrates 2010
An Exhibition in Memory of Constance Sherridan Hefner
Featuring Works by Students, Faculty and Staff
April 5 – May 7, 2010

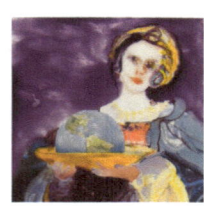

Eric Finzi: Circular Reasoning
An Exhibition of Paintings and Sculpture
May 25 – August 6, 2010

As a curator and printmaker, I often reflect on the past while contemplating future projects. Thinking back on my artistic development, I was fortunate to have generous teachers, prominent and lesser known, who taught discipline and training that rattled my nerves and toughened my stamina. A more difficult lesson was to embrace the talents given and identify one's path, leading me to rely on instinct, hone technique, and execute ideas through a medium that best conveys a concept.

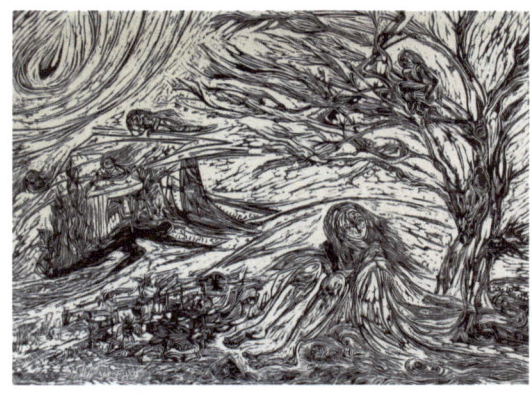

Sensing Loss

My work interweaves training in the fine arts, theatre, and choreography. As a young woman, I witnessed genius while studying with Charles Weidman, the father of modern dance. In college, I experienced aesthetic challenges under the tutelage of Elizabeth Murray. While living in Italy, my Venetian voice teacher, Maestro Ferraris, said something that became a metaphor for my creative life. "Cecilia, you must use the gift God gave you. You cannot sing opera if your voice is suited for 'musica da camera.' You must be yourself and accept the gift given you." These words are with me daily as I've learned to trust myself and execute my work with the eye of a caretaker.

Cecilia Rossey
Guest Curator
2009, 2010, 2012
Artist-in-Residence 2014

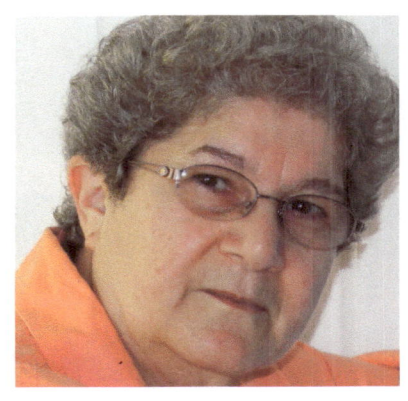

In 2008, after the death of a young friend in Afghanistan, I was motivated by a need to create a "War Memorial: Iraq and Afghanistan," honoring the soldiers killed in the conflict. I approached Deborah Sokolove, curator of the Dadian Gallery, and a meeting progressed to a relationship as guest curator. Over the years, the Dadian Gallery has hosted *An Artist's Reaction to War*, *Food and Form*, and *Black.White.ReAd: Journey Through the Maze*, concept exhibits dealing with issuers relating to war, the politics of food, and finding faith through human crisis. An exhibit in progress, *Votes, Violence, Victory*, honors Suffragettes, those who advocated equality and the right to change law in a democratic society.

The Dadian Gallery is not only a splendid gallery space but has become a welcome home. Works of art are lovingly cared for by the curator and appreciated and accepted by the viewers. Many thanks to Deborah Sokolve, director of the Henry Luce III Center for Arts and Religion, Trudi Ludwig, and Alexandra Sherman, present and former curators, for their various invitations. I am now part of this community and look forward to my experience as an artist-in-residence, artist, and curator, and sharing a version of world issues through artistic my endeavors.

My recent work, dedicated to earth awareness, advocates respect for humans, elements, and creatures alike. We share this earth, as particles of this planet, and must assume and respect our intended role. We cannot place cause and effect in the hands of God alone or using God's will as an excuse for natural disasters. As intelligent beings, we must be better stewards of this earth. While it is necessary to consume, it is also necessary to restore balance. The future existence of earth's bounty is one's responsibility, and assuming that responsibility heightens a natural instinct for preservation. It is unusual to destroy a beautiful design once it is known as treasure.

www.cisrossey.com

2010-2011

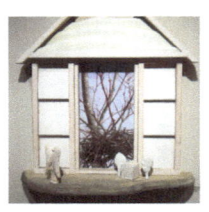

Waiting, Watching, Being...
Collaborative works by
Jennifer L. Collins and Charlie Brouwer
August 23 – October 13, 2010

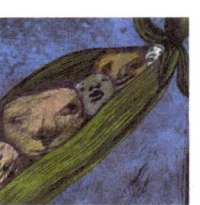

Food and Form
A Group Exhibition with Guest Curator Cecilia Rosey
October 25 – December 17, 2010

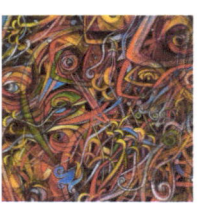

Charis:
Boundary Crossings Neighbors Strangers Family Friends
An International Traveling Exhibition
January 18 – March 4, 2011

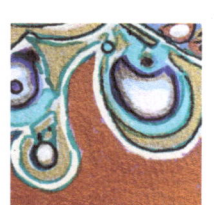

From the Studio: 2009 – 2011 Artists-in-Residence
Carolyn Gass, Cynthia Farrell Johnson, Catherine Kapikian,
Mary Padgelek, Douglas Purnell, Lauren Raine,
and Karen Swenholt
March 28 – May 6, 2011

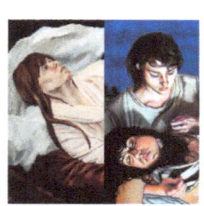

Close: Figurative Works
Paintings by Paul Kehrer and Emma Steinkraus
May 31 – August 5, 2011

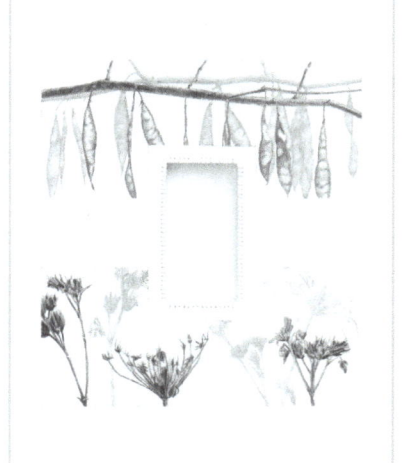

On Beginning Again
from the collection of Glenda Brouwer

Jennifer Leah Hand

Formerly
Jennifer L. Collins
Exhibition 2010

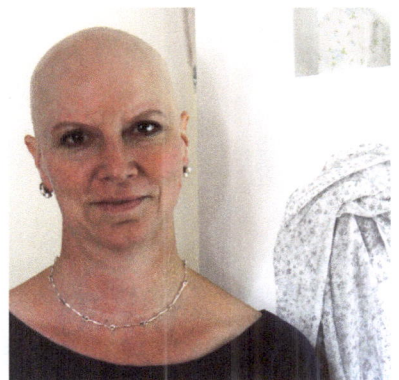

Marrying, moving, building a new studio and rebuilding a home have all contributed to the work I have done since my collaborative exhibition with Charlie Brouwer at the Dadian Gallery in 2010. My recent drawings contemplate themes of transition, balance, and the act of making a place to occupy both physically and spiritually. I find meaning and inspiration through searching for the extraordinary in the ordinary.

I understand the act of making something to be a metaphor for living. There is a time of anticipation and unknowing in the beginning of the process, a stretch of hard work and struggle in the middle, a period of growth and triumph while overcoming that struggle, and a time of reflection at the end. This process is repeated over and over as we live our lives.

While making these recent drawings I have been thinking about this act of living a life and how it propels us forward, stitching us in and out of the spiritual and physical realms as we search for some kind of whole. They feel like fragments that when pieced together may reveal something closer to what that "whole" might be, or…maybe not. Perhaps they simply reveal more of the mystery.

I think this is okay. I think what continues to propel us forward is that we don't have answers. We are all driven by a search for something we can't quite define. We see hints of its glory all around us, if we slow down long enough to look, and this is enough. The truth is, we need the mystery.

2011-2012

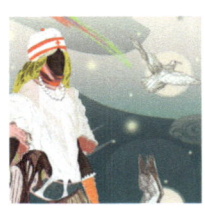

Strength and Struggle: Haiti Continued
Digital Works by Lavar Munroe
August 22 – October 14, 2011

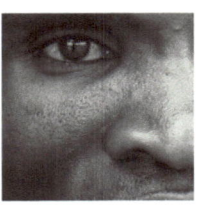

30 years 30 lives
Photography by Kim Vrudny
August 29 – October 14, 2011
In the Board Room

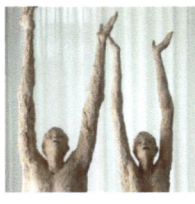

The Dust Cries Out: Twin Tower Memorial
Sculpture by Karen Swenholt
September 2011

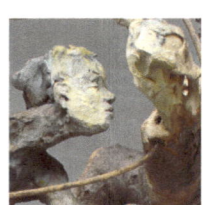

The Seven Deadlies
Sculpture by Karen Swenholt
October 31 – December 16, 2011

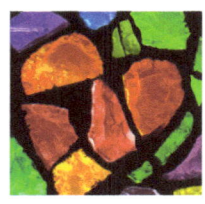

The Seminary Celebrates 2012
An Exhibition in Memory of Constance Sherridan Hefner
Featuring works by students, faculty and staff
January 9 – March 1, 2012
"Heart the Arts Festival" February 14, 2012

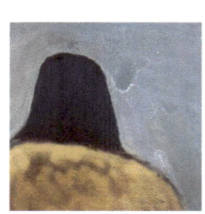

Christ Paintings
by Larry Deyab
March 19 – June 1, 2012

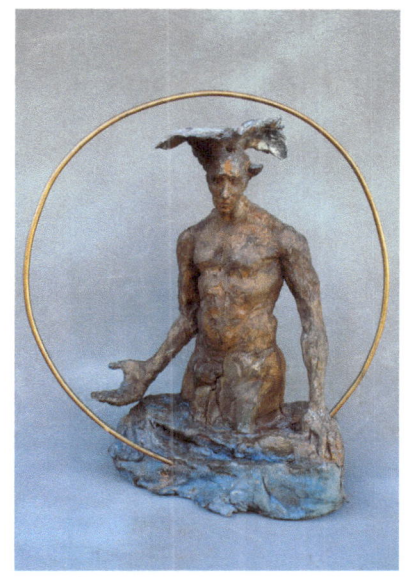

Sacred Water

Karen Swenholt

Exhibition 2011
Artist-in-Residence
2010 – 2011

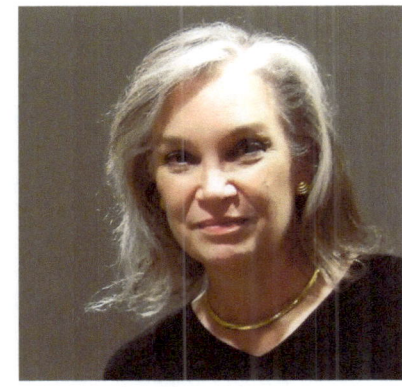

I have met an enlightened few, but generally the art world has little tolerance for Christianity. Art that flows through the supernatural is only celebrated after its impact has been disconnected from its cultural context by time. I appreciate permission to celebrate art of the long-dead faithful but I am greedy to make a contemporary impact. Unfortunately we 21st century Christian artists are like creatures of the Galapagos—detached from the flow of history on irrelevant islands where our churches and seminaries have become ghettos to contain ideas, not propagate them. This is not by choice. I routinely change titles at curator's requests. "Jesus' Baptism" becomes "Sacred Water." It can get creative. The water is not sacred in itself but since the water has touched Him it is ennobled. "The Adulteress and Jesus" becomes "Diptych: Drawing in the Sand and Waiting for the First Stone." Though individual pieces can be trick-titled, suppression forces unified bodies of work into secular themes. Wesley gave me the opportunity to publicly integrate my art and faith through the language of my work. My Dadian solo exhibition, *The Seven Deadlies,* could not even be conceived for a secular gallery. The curators here permitted me open expression. There is an embarrassed void left where God and art once danced publicly. Dadian permitted me that dance and I experienced real creative freedom for the first time in a serious venue. It was a delight to work with people who appreciate art for art's sake and respect that it can be a conduit for the Divine.

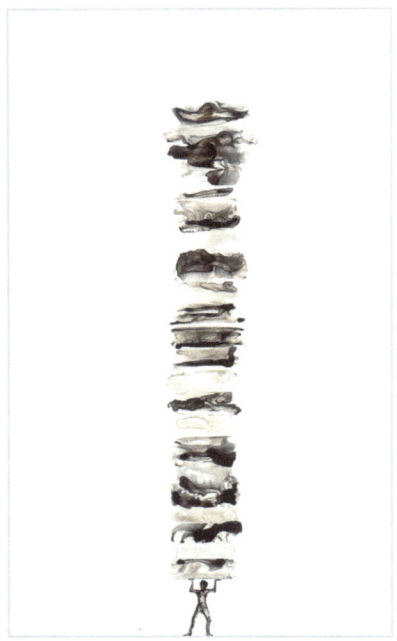

Pre-determination

Alexandra N. Sherman

Curator, 2009 – 2012
Artist-in-Residence
2010 & 2013 – 2014

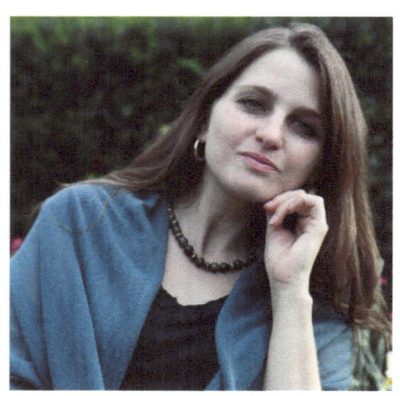

My first response to art is always physical, and perhaps it is right that it not be immediately translated into the realm of words. It is only later that I am able to put words to what I have seen, and yet as if a foreign translation, something is lost.

As an artist and a curator I seek to evoke a visceral response within the viewer, whether it be an unconscious smile forming upon the lips or an uneasiness of the stomach.

The glass front of the Dadian Gallery acts as a jewel case within the Kresge building, inviting the Wesley community and visitors to take a moment and step into a different space and mindset. The Dadian is much like a chapel, a space set aside for the purpose of reflection. The gallery challenges us to engage in the act of looking and to use a different and often underutilized sense to illuminate the world and to better understand our place within it.

www.ansherman.com

Whether contextualizing the creative experience, or unpacking technical, intellectual, and spiritual processes of art making, a Dadian Gallery exhibition provides an opportunity to educate both its audience *and* its artists. As a curator and educator, I believe that both audience and artist should learn from the process of creativity, and that the two are inseparable. This is especially true when art tackles the spiritual.

Many contemporary artists consider themselves spiritual beings, but are reluctant to admit that their work is faith-based or to accept the label 'religious.' This is not surprising. Acknowledging the sacred as a creative impulse has largely been marginalized by the mainstream and academic art world for several decades.

For the past 25 years, exhibitions in the Dadian Gallery have offered work arriving at the crossroads of art and faith. The slip and spark of creative energies colliding at that intersection are as miraculous as the moment of conception, producing a ripple effect with the potential to resonate into the community outside the walls of the Seminary. Dadian artists draw from the reservoir of the sacred in order to discover, delve into, and reveal personal truths, giving visual life to the world's great faith traditions. Though the content of their work may trouble the waters, challenge contemporary art world norms, or resurrect neglected art forms, Dadian artists' visual mediations offer a brave and profound exploration of inward self-knowledge even as their chosen materials and images challenge viewers to scrutinize their own spiritual lives.

Not only has the Dadian investigated, invited, celebrated, and showcased the work of established artists, it is also fully committed to nurturing visual seekers and emerging artists *of all ages*, empowering them to find and raise their voices, so the practice of their faith may be fully integrated into their studio practice. The Dadian Gallery experience becomes an effective ministry: to comfort the challenged, and challenge the comfortable. In this way, confusion leads to learning and new meanings come to life. Work presented in the Dadian is an art of worth and service for both the artists and the audience.

With the wealth of experience earned over the past 25 years, we embolden our mission to weave the transformative power of the Dadian's treasures into the fabric of the wider world. May all who see be embraced by the creative spirit. Onward!

www.ludwigprints.com

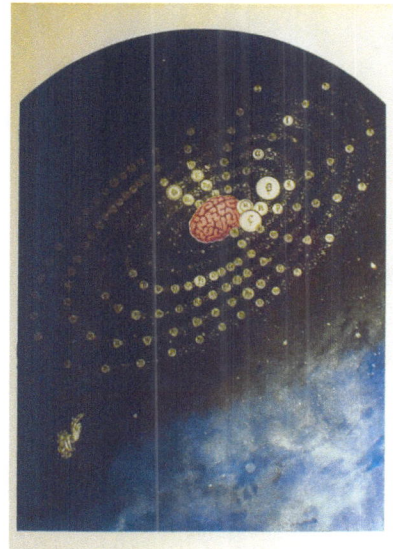
Dumb Luck

Trudi Y. Ludwig

Curator, 2012 – Present
Exhibition 2007
Artist-in-Residence 2012

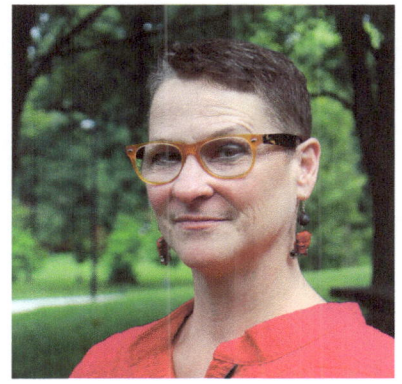

2012-2013

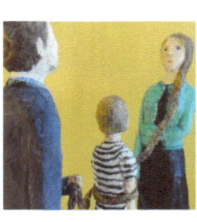

The Paper People
Papier-mâché Sculpture by Rosemary Markowski
June 18 – September 26, 2012

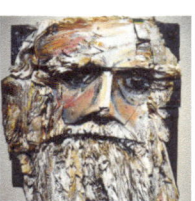

BLACK.WHITE.REaD: Journey Through the Maze
An Invitational Group Exhibition
with Guest Curator Cecilia Rossey
October 15 – December 14, 2012

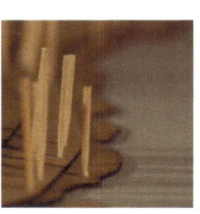

Box of Miracles: Contemplating a 21st Century Convent
Architectural Drawings and Models from the Sacred Space
and Cultural Studies Concentration at Catholic University
of America School of Architecture and Planning
January 23 – March 1, 2013

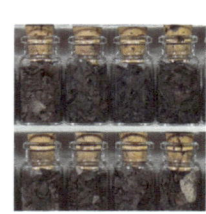

Paul Roorda: Rites & Remedies
Repurposed Bibles and Other Constructions
March 13 – May 24, 2013

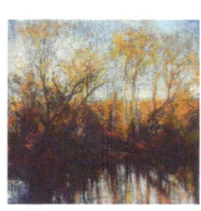

River - Flow - Light
Paintings and Drawings by Dale Jones
An Exhibition in Honor of Trever Bennet
June 10 – August 9, 2013

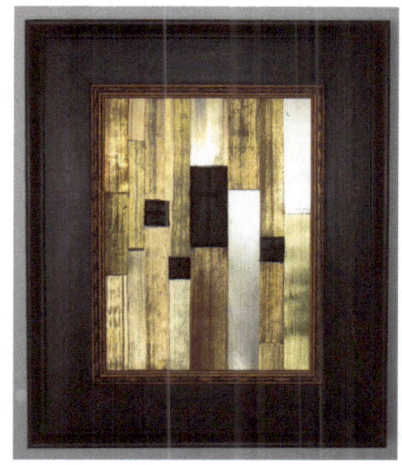

Icon VI

Paul Roorda
Exhibition 2013

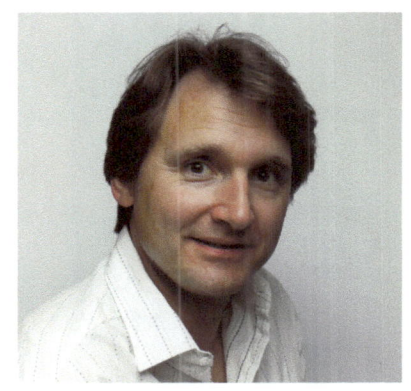

Showing my work at the Dadian was a highlight for me in recent years. After working for over a decade with a focus on religious beliefs and ritual, having an exhibition at the Dadian was an opportunity to show a collection of work that included the many approaches I have taken while exploring this topic. Over the years, I found myself going deeper and deeper into unraveling ideas about the place of ritual in religious and human experience and the way beliefs are held firmly or abandoned in an attempt to know some kind of truth.

I appreciated the openness of the curators of the Dadian Gallery to exhibit work that is meant to challenge the viewer on both emotional and intellectual levels. People's experience of faith is often not easy, and my goal is to make art that reflects the complexities of human experience of religion. Decisions around what truth to believe, what actions are morally right, or what rituals have value, come with conflicting emotions. The ritualized process I use in creating art from discarded Bibles is an attempt to cut to the heart of these issues, and by exposing and pulling back layers of meaning create new understanding. It felt like my art had found a temporary home at the Dadian Gallery, a place where the experience and discussion it created was welcome.

My exhibition at the Dadian was more than just about ideas though. I was struck by the visual beauty of the gallery and the way it could hold my work up in its light. As an exhibition space, it really is a jewel. Its intimate size worked very well for my small sculptures and yet the openness of the glass front was a visually welcoming invitation to experience the art. And as much as I enjoy the conceptual quality of art, I love the beauty, the theatre, and the mystery of art as well. In the Dadian Gallery, I was able to see my own work in new light, as a viewer as well as a creator, and that was a gift.

www.paulroorda.com

2013-2014

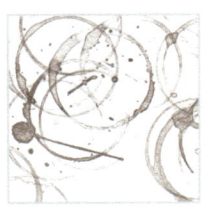

Our Lady of Perpetual Exhaustion
An Invitational Exhibition with the Watergate Gallery
August 27 – October 4, 2013

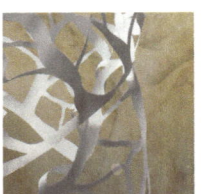

Amy E. Gray: The Extravagant Gift
An Installation of Silverpoint Drawings and Paper Lace
October 21 – January 10, 2014

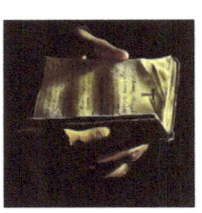

Lineage
Paintings by Matthew Adelberg
January 20 – March 7, 2014

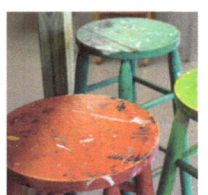

From the Studio: Artists-in-Residence 2011-2014
Barbara Green, Cynthia Farrell Johnson, Geraldine Kiefer,
Trudi Y. Ludwig, Maureen Melville, Margaret Adams
Parker, Alexandra N. Sherman, and Emma Steinkraus
March 17 – June 6, 2014

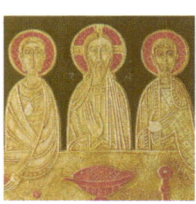

Living Tradition: Icons for the Liturgical Year
by Philip Davydov and Olga Shalamova
June 17 – September 19, 2014

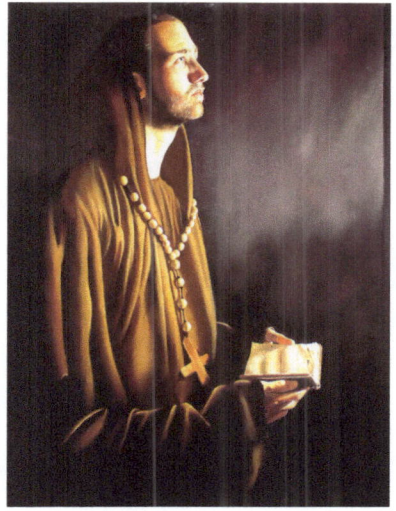

St Francis

Matthew Adelberg
Exhibition 2014

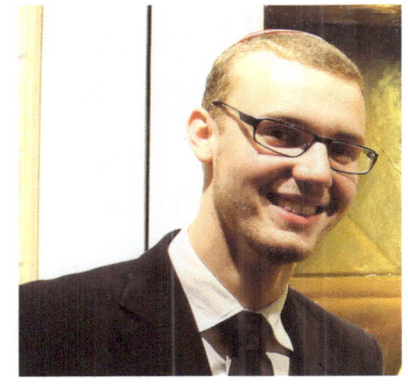

When asked to write about what showing at the Dadian Gallery has meant to me, so many things came to mind. I could talk about meeting a childhood idol, the largest living influence on my artwork. I could talk about how, as a result of being given the opportunity to show here, I got to spend two months in Norway. I could talk about being commissioned by the family of one of my favorite artists, Andrew Wyeth. But I realize that regardless of the tangible success that the show brought me, regardless of the miles I got to travel, regardless of the future opportunities I have been given, the most important thing the Dadian Gallery gave to me was confidence in myself as an artist and person of faith. My time so far with the Dadian Gallery has taught me that being an artist and an extremely faithful person are not different, separate things. But rather, they are intertwined and inseparable. Showing at the Dadian Gallery instilled in me a deeper understanding of the relationship between art and faith. The experience allowed me to understand that the process of making art and the process of practicing my faith are one and the same. Through this enlightenment, I have found myself stronger in my faith, more devoted to my artwork, and more capable of finding light in the dark. For this I could not be more grateful.

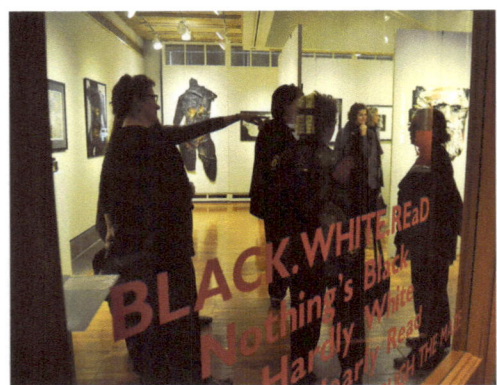
Guests in the gallery, 2012

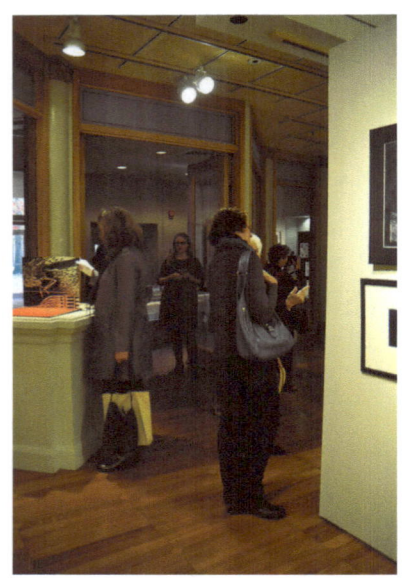
Guests in the gallery, 2012

Thank You

It takes more than the artists and curators involved in keeping the gallery running smoothly for 25 years, far more than we can possibly name. We would like to thank: Catherine Kapikian, for her initial vision for the gallery and her contribution of archival material about the early days of the Henry Luce III Center for the Arts and Religion; past President G. Douglass Lewis, for his courage in establishing it; President David McAllister-Wilson, for inviting us to extend the gallery experience into his office and his patient willingness to learn more about what makes good art; Deans Bruce Birch, Amy Oden, and Robert Martin, for their enthusiastic support of all the arts during each of their tenures; Juyeon Jeon and all of the other student workers who have assisted in a variety of ways through the years; Raymond Washington and his staff in the mailroom; Amy Shelton, Lyndon Orinion, and others who have worked on marketing; Jane Deland, Chip Aldridge, Diane Wogaman, Nehemias Molinas, Oscar Palencia, Luis Claros, Amelia Masdin, Josie Hoover, Desiree Barnes, Sage Dining, everyone else who has encouraged and helped us by attending our exhibitions and artist talks, writing on our "comments" pages, asking to be put on our mailing list, or opening doors when our hands were filled with packages and pedestals; and anyone who we have forgotten to list but nonetheless deserves our gratitude. We want to extend a very special thank you to all of the spouses, partners, family and friends that have supported our artists, and transported their work over the last 25 years! Most importantly, thank you to Randall Adams who gets the last word on anything that goes up on the walls anywhere on campus.

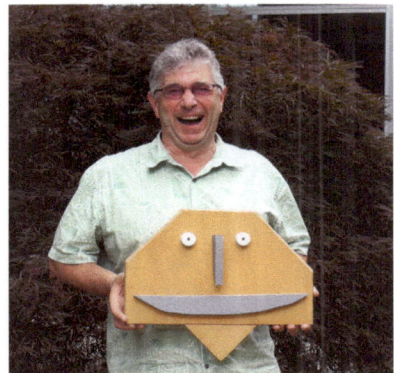

New Life for Leftover Forms

The Last Word

After 25 years of working with the Center for Arts and Religion, I am humbled at what to say and how to express my feelings about my experience here. I came to the Seminary in August of 1988 in the midst of the Kresge renovation, and was involved from the very beginning with the CAR. My first task was to make sure that the Gallery did not flood after torrential rains in late August and early September, especially since the elevator had no roof. I can remember Dr. Lewis and I diverting water away from the newly laid gallery floor to the outside via an old piece of gutter and a large trash can. There were some tense moments there. We have come a long way since those early days. I have been blessed and very fortunate to have, for the past 25 years, been involved with hanging and lighting EVERY show that has been displayed in that space. The CAR and I have not only presented shows in the Gallery, but have branched out to the entire campus. I have hung practically every work of art around our campus.

Randall Adams

Director of Facilities
Art Installer
Extraordinaire
1988 – Present

The man behind the magic

I have learned a lot over the years from the artists themselves and the wonderful CAR staff. It has always been fun and challenging to work with all the different curators as we put our heads together to figure out the best gallery presentation to highlight an artist's work. At the successful presentation/hanging of each show there is a magnificent rush that comes over the curator, the artist, and me, as if we won a race. The shows have been breathtaking. I am proud and honored to have been a part of this exceptional program here at Wesley Seminary. I also have one of my own creations displayed in the printer room of the Business Office. Art can be addictive.

I look forward to working and enjoying my remaining years supporting the CAR.

Randall

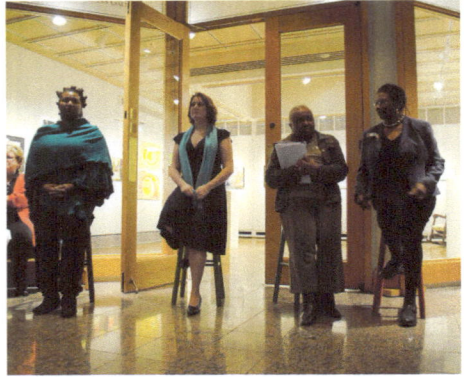
Students perform outside the gallery, 2012

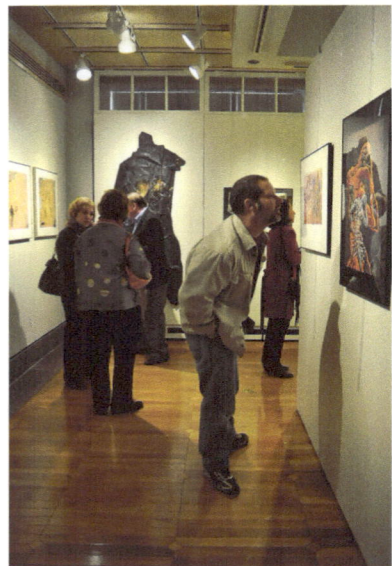
Guests in the gallery, 2012

Contributers

Photo credits:

Images of individual artists and their works are courtesy of the artist unless otherwise noted. Exhibition photos are courtesy of the Henry Luce III Center for the Arts and Religion staff. We are grateful to the photographers whose names we were unable to discover by the time of publication, and apologize for any omissions or errors in giving proper credit.